The essays in ... W9-APO-122
power Problems," examine the difficulties confronting the hard-to-employ in their attempt to gain a toehold in a metropolitan economy. The contributors assess implications of the changing educational requirements for employment, the obstacles faced by young workers who are not college-bound, and the problems of the peripheral worker. The experiences of the countries of Western Europe in their efforts to provide opportunities for the hard-to-employ are described.

In Part Three, "Potential and Policy," the chapters are focused on the future of the metropolis and its continued growth. The unrealized potential of educated women, the close link between the economy and higher education, and public policies conducive to economic expansion are stressed.

In the concluding chapter, Professor Ginzberg draws upon the important suggestions contained in the several chapters and delineates a manpower strategy for the metropolis.

Eli Ginzberg is Hepburn Professor of Economics and Director of the Conservation of Human Resources Project at Columbia University. Individual chapters were contributed by Thomas M. Stanback Jr., Boris Yavitz, Harry I. Greenfield, Carol A. Brown, Ivar E. Berg, Marcia K. Freedman, Dean W. Morse, Beatrice G. Reubens, Alice M. Yohalem, Dale L. Hiestand, and Alfred E. Eichner.

Printed in U.S.A.

Manpower Strategy for the Metropolis

Manpower Strategy for the Metropolis

by *Eli Ginzberg* and
The Conservation of Human Resources Staff,
Columbia University

Columbia University Press
New York and London   1968

Copyright © 1968 Columbia University Press
Library of Congress Catalog Card Number: 68-27290
Printed in the United States of America

Preface

The Conservation of Human Resources Project, Columbia University, has been engaged in research in human resources and manpower since the late 1930s. But it was not until the last few years that it began to direct part of its efforts to regional and local problems.

This volume, which presents the results of one of several studies which the Conservation Project has been conducting for the New York City Planning Commission, was designed to distill important lessons for the future planning of New York City and, by implication, other large metropolitan centers from manpower investigations that initially had a broader focus.

This attempt to reconcile a national with a local perspective reflects our desire to respond to the request of the Planning Commission for guidance and our growing conviction that many of the more intractable manpower problems facing the nation—such as the need to improve articulation between the educational system and the world of work and the need to reduce the gap between workers without skills and the search of employers for competence—can be properly assessed and effectively resolved only by a more encompassing approach.

While many manpower issues can be planned and executed only at a national level, other critically important dimensions of manpower have an overwhelming local hue, such as where people are born, the neighborhoods in which they grow up, the schools they attend, and the jobs to which they have access. This underlines the importance of developing a strategy for the metropolis.

This book is a collaborative effort by twelve members of the Conservation staff. A major research investigation provides the basis for each chapter. The bibliography provides the details about larger investigations, both those that have recently been published and those which will become available in the near future. Because this book rests so heavily on antecedent research, recognition is given to the sponsors of the earlier work: the Manpower Administration of the U.S. Department of Labor, the Center for Urban Education, the Russell Sage Foundation, the Rockefeller Brothers Fund, and the New York City Planning Commission.

Since its inception the Conservation Project has planned its research along a limited number of axes. However, since the staff has been drawn from different disciplines, the result has inevitably been one of some diversity within a broadly united approach. The observant reader will note differences in perspective and emphasis and even contradiction in the chapters which follow. I have deliberately avoided camouflaging or eliminating their differences on the assumption that it is better that the reader note we differ among ourselves than that we pretend to a spurious agreement. Since this book has been shaped from the basic research which the Conservation Project has had under way, certain emphasis and omissions have followed.

The Introduction was written to provide the reader with

an orientation to the specific manpower problems of New York City as well as to outline the substantive treatments which follow. The concluding chapter, drawing on the important suggestions contained in the several chapters, seeks to delineate a manpower strategy for the metropolis.

It is not easy to make one book out of the work of twelve authors. To the extent that this has been accomplished is largely the result of the editorial contribution of Ruth S. Ginzberg.

ELI GINZBERG
Director, Conservation of
Human Resources Project

Columbia University
January, 1968

Contents

Manpower Strategy for the Metropolis

INTRODUCTION

Metropolitan Perspective

THIS introductory chapter has three objectives. It will present certain basic facts about the important changes that have been affecting the people who live within the New York metropolitan area. It will highlight some of the major changes in the structure of business, particularly with regard to the jobs that are available within the region. And it will furnish an overview of the chapters which comprise this book so that the reader can see at the outset the dynamic changes in the economic life of the metropolis that, in our opinion, have such momentous consequences for the development and utilization of the city's manpower resources.

In the decade of the 1950s the population of New York City ceased to grow. The Census of 1960 showed a total of 7.782 million people in New York City, or roughly 110,000 less than the 7.892 million counted in 1950. Although estimates for the mid-1960s indicate a modest increase, it appears that the city proper is not likely to expand in the near future much beyond the 8 million mark.

Within this relatively stable total, marked changes have occurred in the groups which comprise it. The most striking changes during the 1950s were the exodus of the white population to the suburbs and the less but still substantial in-migration of Negroes and Puerto Ricans. When these migration figures are added to the changes brought about by births and deaths, we find that the city lost 837,000 whites and gained about 727,000 Negroes and Puerto Ricans in about equal number.

There are no definite data available for the intercensal years of the 1960s. The information which does exist points to the following: a substantial slowing up in the flight of whites from the city paralleled by a marked reduction in Negro and Puerto Rican in-migrants. But because of the substantially younger age distribution of the latter two groups and their relatively high birth rates, the proportion of the white population to the total continues to decline. The 1970 Census will probably reveal that more than 1 out of every 4 New Yorkers is either a Negro or a Puerto Rican with one and a half as many Negroes as Puerto Ricans.

In a society which by law, if not in fact, is supposed to be color-blind, why do we put so much emphasis on identifying the changes in the city's population according to racial-ethnic groupings? The answer is simple. These designations provide a shorthand for other critically important variables that will largely determine the well-being of the population as well as the present economic condition and future prospects of the metropolis.

The Negro and the Puerto Rican in-migrants tend to be less educated and less skilled than the native-born whites and accordingly must compete for the least attractive jobs. In turn, they earn less, live in poorer neighborhoods, and are not able to provide their children with the opportunities required for the full development of their potential. In addition, the Puerto Rican in-migrant must learn a new language. And many Negro in-migrants find it difficult to establish and maintain a stable family structure, with the result that their children grow up without adequate parental supervision, and this in turn militates against their sound emotional and intellectual development.

Although the in-migrant is particularly handicapped, inadequate education, low skills, poor jobs, low incomes, and slum living also characterize many members of these two minority groups who were born and brought up in New York. They have been unable to rise above the disadvantages and deprivations that have been part of their environment since they were born.

In brief then, a substantial proportion of native-born and in-migrant Negroes and Puerto Ricans are poorly educated, have only modest skills, and are not able to compete successfully for the better jobs that New York has to offer. They are condemned to poverty and deprivation, and they represent a drag on the vitality and growth of the city's economy by failing to add to the pool of skills and by forcing the city to spend large sums on relief.

But it would be an error to exaggerate the magnitude of this problem just as it would be an error to ignore it. Even today these two disadvantaged minorities comprise less than a quarter of the city's population. Moreover not all, or even most, of the Negro and Puerto Rican families in the city are trapped in poverty.

However, the minority poor do pose a threat to the well-being and vitality of the city. A distressingly high proportion of minority youth fail to achieve at grade level at the end of elementary school and only a very small proportion of them complete academic high school, which would place them in a preferred position to enter white-collar occupations.

On the other hand, we will see that the New York economy continues to have a large number of job openings for blue-collar and service workers who do not have to demonstrate a high order of competence in the communication arts, mathematics, or analytical skills. Moreover, employers in New York City do not have to draw their labor force solely from among the residents of the city.

Of the approximately 2 million persons who work in mid-Manhattan, south of 60th Street, about 400,000—or 1 in 5—commute to work from outside the city. While the proportions of males to females among the 2 million is about 55 to 45 percent, the proportion of males to females among commuters is 75 to 25 percent. The commuters, especially the men, include many with managerial, technical, and other skills which contribute to the vitality of the city's economy.

In 1960, the population of the New York metropolitan region was approximately 16 million persons. For every person living within the city there was one outside the city limits whose life was affected by what transpired in the major metropolis at the center of the area. The critical importance of the city is here illustrated by the distribution of employment throughout the area. In January, 1966, there were approximately 5 million employed persons in the metropolitan area of whom about 3.9 million—or just under 80 percent—earned their livelihood within the city.

The work profile of the city is presented in Table 1, which sets out the employment within New York City during the period 1947–1965. The following points are worthy of note. The total number of jobs expanded only slightly— about 8 percent—during the past fifteen years. But within this stable total, significant changes occurred. The manufacturing sector showed a substantial decline, both in

durable and nondurable goods, but with a much more pronounced decline in the nondurable sector. Nevertheless,
manufacturing accounted for the single largest aggregation
of jobs in 1965. Employment slipped off in a few important
manufacturing areas, such as machinery, transportation
equipment, food, apparel, and leather products but with
866,000 jobs in manufacturing in 1965 the city's manufacturing base was still impressive.

The 285,000 jobs that were added in the nonmanufacturing sector of the economy during the same period were contained primarily in services, government, and, to a lesser
extent, finance, insurance, and real estate.

Note should be taken of the fact that employment in
three sectors—contract construction, transportation and
public utilities, and wholesale and retail trade, which together accounted for half of all nonmanufacturing employment in 1950—had actually declined by 1965. When this
fact is put together with the trend in manufacturing employment, an important conclusion emerges. The jobs
which poorly educated in-migrants and native-born with
limited skills could most readily fill did not expand. In fact
the number of such jobs actually declined. Herein lies one
of the severe pressure fronts. Many residents in New York
City are not prepared for the jobs that are expanding. Were
it not that employers located within the city have been able
to draw on people who live in the larger metropolitan area,
many of whom are willing to travel long distances to work,
the economy of the city might have been in jeopardy.

Challenges remain. As large numbers of middle-class
white families relocated in the suburbs and in exurbia,
many businesses—manufacturing plants, wholesaling and
warehousing operations, department stores, company head-

Table 1. Employment in New York City, by Industry, 1947–1965 (in thousands)

Industry	1965	1960	1950	1947	Changes for Selected Periods 1947–65	1950–60	1960–65
Total	3,581.0	3,538.4	3,468.2	n.a.	n.a.	+70.2	+42.6
MANUFACTURING	866.4	946.8	1,038.9	1,072.9	−206.5	−92.1	−80.4
Durable Goods	272.6	303.6	310.9	328.1	−55.5	−7.3	−31.0
Ordnance and accessories	1.8	4.2	n.a.	n.a.	n.a.	n.a.	−2.4
Lumber and wood products (except furniture)	5.7	6.0	7.2	7.7	−2.0	−1.2	−0.3
Furniture and fixtures	17.8	17.7	22.6	20.7	−2.9	−4.9	+0.1
Stone, clay, and glass products	9.7	11.3	12.4	12.0	−2.3	−1.1	−1.6
Primary metal industries	14.1	13.4	14.4	13.3	+0.8	−1.0	+0.7
Fabricated metal products	39.6	44.4	n.a.	n.a.	n.a.	n.a.	−4.8
Machinery (except electrical)	30.4	35.2	31.8	40.0	−9.6	+3.4	−4.8
Electrical equipment and supplies	49.5	60.3	52.6	51.7	−2.2	+7.7	−10.8
Transportation equipment	10.4	11.7	14.9	27.1	−16.7	−3.2	−1.3
Instruments and related products	23.0	24.2	26.1	27.1	−4.1	−1.9	−1.2
Miscellaneous manufacturing	70.5	75.1	80.6	79.5	−9.0	−5.5	−4.6
Nondurable Goods	593.7	643.2	727.9	744.7	−151.0	−84.7	−49.5
Food and kindred products	67.4	81.6	98.3	102.9	−35.5	−16.7	−14.2

Tobacco manufactures	2.7	2.7	4.0	4.2	−1.5	−1.3	—
Textile mill products	35.3	36.1	38.5	35.7	−0.4	−2.4	−0.8
Apparel and related products	242.9	267.4	340.7	349.0	−106.1	−73.3	−24.5
Paper and related products	27.5	30.2	28.5	28.4	−0.9	+1.7	−2.7
Printing, publishing, and allied industries	126.3	127.2	119.2	121.5	+4.8	+8.0	−0.9
Chemicals and allied products	43.4	45.9	42.3	46.5	−3.1	+3.6	−2.5
Petroleum refining and related products	7.3	9.9	8.2	7.2	+0.1	+1.7	−2.6
Rubber and miscellaneous products	11.7	10.5	10.8	9.8	+1.9	−0.3	+1.2
Leather and leather products	29.2	31.6	37.4	39.5	−10.3	−5.8	−2.4
NONMANUFACTURING	2,714.6	2,591.6	2,429.3	n.a.	n.a.	+162.3	+123.0
Mining	2.4	1.9	1.7	n.a.	n.a.	+0.2	+0.5
Contract construction	109.2	125.3	123.0	n.a.	n.a.	+2.3	−16.1
Transportation and public utilities	319.1	318.1	331.5	n.a.	n.a.	−13.4	+1.0
Wholesale and retail trade	747.9	744.8	754.8	n.a.	n.a.	−10.0	+3.1
Finance, insurance, and real estate	393.7	386.0	336.2	n.a.	n.a.	+49.8	+7.7
Service and miscellaneous	681.1	607.3	507.7	n.a.	n.a.	+99.6	+73.8
Government	461.2	408.2	374.4	n.a.	n.a.	+33.8	+53.0

quarters, and a host of service establishments—have followed in their wake. Some businesses have moved to be closer to a preferred labor supply; others have been attracted by the availability of land; still others have wanted to be free of the dangers and difficulties that have come to characterize urban existence: poor transportation; dirty streets; lack of personal safety.

The following chapters provide significant perspectives on the strengths and weaknesses of large cities and contain a host of suggestions as to how they can maintain the lead which they assumed some decades ago as pacesetters in every realm of national life—economic, social, and cultural. The unity of these several chapters is that each one is addressed to the role of the human resource factor in metropolitan economies. This does not imply that the other parameters of economic life—space, technology, location, finances—are unimportant; however, the vitality of advanced economics depends increasingly on the quality of the population—their drive, knowledge, competence, leadership, and ability to work together.

The chapters in Part One are concerned with how metropolitan economies can keep themselves vital. The analysis begins with a demonstration of the fact that one important dimension of competition in the United States is intensive rivalry among large cities. The data indicate that since 1950, the largest cities, those with over 3 million people, have found it difficult to retain their lead over cities with a population of one million. It appears that important forces are at work which make it difficult for the very large cities to continue to achieve further economies of scale and to avoid the diseconomies of size.

Part of the explanation for this differential rate of growth over the last two decades which has given the edge to the cities that are not yet megalopoli is the impact of the new technology which is reducing the dependence of cities on proximity to raw materials or markets. Another explanation is the greater ease with which smaller metropolitan centers can fashion and refashion public policy to respond to the changes in technology both defensively, to protect enterprises that have been made vulnerable, and offensively, to exploit the potentialities inherent in a new technology.

Whether the economies of cities grow, remain stable, or even decline is also a function of the strength of their producer services. Here the very large cities have a clear advantage. Basic to economic growth and profitability is increased specialization. Whether firms can increase their specialization hinges on the range and quality of the producer services available to them. The larger the city, the greater the availability of producer services. But, as often happens, the trend moves in two directions. While it is easier for a firm to slough off extraneous activities when strong producer services are available and to buy rather than to produce them, this means that many producer firms become established and expand, thereby adding an important dimension to the city's growth. Producer services account for almost 25 percent of the gross national product; they make use of large numbers of trained persons who earn good incomes; and they represent a precondition for maintaining a high level of economic activity.

The last chapter in Part One presents "Health Services" as a case study of a rapidly growing sector of urban employment. In *The Pluralistic Economy* (1964), we called attention to a new phenomenon: at least 1 out of 3 workers are employed in the not-for-profit sector—that is, in government, nonprofit organizations, or defense companies producing exclusively for government account.

"Health Services" is one of the largest sectors of employment and is exceeded only by agriculture and construction. It is also one of the fastest growing industries; it has had a 60 percent increase in each of the last two decades. New York City has about 210,000 health workers, who represent roughly 5.5 percent of the city's labor force. Health service employment is particularly important since it provides jobs for people with limited education. While in the past many of these jobs paid little, minimum wages are now being rapidly raised through legislation and trade union activity. Moreover, many women from minority groups have obtained work in the health field as technicians with adequate salaries and status. New York City, which has the largest medical complex in the world, has a clear competitive advantage in the health field.

The four chapters in Part Two are concerned with the difficulties confronting the hard-to-employ in their attempt to gain a toehold in a metropolitan economy. The analysis begins with consideration of the changing educational requirements for employment that have characterized the United States during the past quarter-century and the implications of these changes for New York City. Documented action is presented to establish the claim that while changing technology has been reflected in higher skill requirements in certain sectors, the new educational requirements cannot be validated by changes on the factory floor or in the office. The analysis suggests that much of the rise in educational requirements is spurious in that a loose labor market has made it possible for employers to set higher demands while the educational background required for the work has remained the same. In a metropolitan center such as New York, with its large numbers of native-born inhabitants and in-migrants with little effective schooling, the recent tendency to raise educational requirements without justification has been a particularly heavy burden on the most vulnerable part of the population in search of work.

The argument continues with an assessment of the problems found by young workers who are not college-bound— that is, the large numbers who must go to work or into the Armed Services after they complete high school or even before they graduate. These young people are poorly prepared for the task of finding a job and even less well prepared to evolve a career. Some find jobs through which they can acquire skills which will provide them with some occupational mobility. Others obtain employment with large employers whose jobs are so structured that a young person starting at the bottom has an opportunity to advance. But a great many other entrants into the labor force must take whatever jobs they can find, and many of these jobs and work settings lead nowhere. They become marginal workers in marginal jobs.

Chapter 6 suggests policy directions for these undirected workers. The next chapter is concerned with "The Peripheral Worker"—a young person, an older woman, a member of a minority group, or a retired man who does not work full time throughout the year. While some prefer to work less than full-time throughout the year, such as the young person who combines work with study, the mature woman who must run her home while holding a job, and the older man who is no longer physically able to work full time but who does not want to be idle—while these subgroups are peripheral workers by choice, a great many others are in this category because they have no choice. Some hold a firm place in the economy; others have lost their jobs and cannot find another. They work when they can at any job they can. Since they tend to be handicapped in one or another way, and frequently in multiple ways, they are the last to be hired, the first to be fired. Their employment records are interspersed with periods of unemployment. The many peripheral workers—who represent about 45 percent of all who have work experience during the course of a year— reflect not only personal preferences or weaknesses but also the pattern of staffing that has come to characterize large sectors of the economy outside of manufacturing and the civil service. The large service arena—which today accounts for the majority of jobs, and which is continuing to grow at the expense of the goods-producing sector—is heavily dependent on part-time workers.

The last chapter in Part Two draws on the experience of the countries of Western Europe in their efforts to provide opportunities for the hard-to-employ. This chapter tells us that all of the countries in Western Europe have had labor shortages since 1950, and as a consequence they have designed a great many policies and programs aimed at helping handicapped workers to keep their jobs. Europe has a less sophisticated technology than ours, which means that there are relatively more jobs for men with few skills. Moreover, they do not have large racial and ethnic minorities who have recently left the farm and must now find a place in a complex metropolitan society. Nevertheless, Europe's experience has many suggestions applicable to our own problems.

In Part Three, the chapters are focused on the potentialities of the metropolis for continued growth. One presentation reviews an important manpower resource in all large cities—educated women who are interested in working at least part time but may need some assistance if their valuable education and training is to be put to productive use. About two-fifths of all college students are women. Almost all of them will marry at some time. Many acquire their baccalaureate and even one or more higher degrees before they marry, while others marry and start a family before they complete their formal education. Once they marry and start a family most women find it difficult to hold a full-time or even a part-time job. But as soon as their youngest child enters school, and sometimes before, many women are ready to return to work, if only on a reduced schedule.

Employers in the metropolis are constantly seeking talent and competence. Educated women represent a major pool that has not been effectively tapped in any large American city. Part of the difficulty rests with the rigidity of employers who are reluctant to make any adjustment in their work schedules. Part lies with the inflexibility of educational and training institutions that have demonstrated little interest in the special refresher needs of this large potential work force. And part lies with the educated women themselves, many of whom cannot resolve their ambivalence toward their many options. As a consequence many are unable to clarify their goals and balance their responsibilities at home with those at work.

But the urban economy that wants to remain in the vanguard must take advantage of its under-utilized resources represented by educated women. The modern economy and higher education have become closely linked. Without large numbers of trained generalists and specialists no city, region, or country is likely to remain in the forefront or move there. New York City is particularly fortunate in the wealth of its many higher educational institutions, which assure that employers can recruit large numbers of educated and trained persons. And New York has always been able to attract large numbers of persons who were trained outside the region so that, after taking account of those whom it trains but who locate elsewhere, it has a net balance.

The elaborate structure of higher education in New York City also contributes to the upgrading of the work force by enabling a great many workers to continue their studies part time. In addition new linkages have been formed between business management and the academic world and between the industrial and the academic laboratories. The density of corporate headquarters and institutions of higher learning in the city facilitates these linkages. And more can be done to exploit this important potential. Finally, we must take into account the fact that higher education itself is a major growth industry which provides considerable employment and income both directly and indirectly. As we look ahead, the city with a superior educational plant will be in a preferred competitive situation.

In the last chapter, "Public Policy for Growth," emphasis is placed on the fact that the vitality of the urban economy will in large measure be determined by the wisdom that is exercised in the political arena. No modern urban economy can prosper unless the decisions that are made in the political arena are conducive to continuing economic growth. But it is difficult for politicians to understand the directions which will advance the long-run interests of the city, and even more difficult for them to balance off the forces that are pressing for current benefits, even though yielding to them may hasten the economic decline of the area.

The chapter calls attention to the key factors that have given New York City its comparative advantage—as transportation nucleus, business capital, and cultural center—and the importance of safeguarding and underpinning each of them. Of critical importance is the husbanding of the scarcest of all New York City's scarce resources—its land —and assuring that its policies aim at encouraging the highest possible output of value added per square foot of space. The analysis recognizes the difficulties of the city's pursuing an economic policy of its own without effectively integrating it with the broader policies affecting the region with which it is so intimately related. The future of New York, as of other large metropolises, may well depend on the speed with which effective planning mechanisms are developed to help guide the policy makers both within the central city and the region. It is becoming increasingly clear that the vitality of the city and the vitality of the region are ineluctably linked and that one cannot prosper without the other.

Part One

Economic Framework

New York City within a System of Cities

Basic employment statistics reveal that cities vary widely in terms of size, distribution of their employment among the various industrial classifications, and rates of growth.

There are 214 urban complexes known as standard metropolitan statistical areas (SMSA's) within the American economy. In addition, there are 154 other cities with 25,000 or more persons. These SMSA's and the other cities form a rough hierarchy according to size, with New York City standing at the apex:

Size of SMSA [a] *by Population*	*Number of SMSA's*
more than 6,400,000	1
3,200,001 to 6,400,000	5
1,600,001 to 3,200,000	7
800,001 to 1,600,000	17
400,001 to 800,000	39
200,001 to 400,000	58
100,001 to 200,000	65
25,001 to 100,000 [a]	176

[a] Includes non-SMSA counties with cities of more than 25,000 population.

On the basis of structure of employment (i.e., the distribution of employment among the various industrial classifications such as manufacturing, retailing, wholesaling, finance, education, and health services), cities fall into three general categories. One category, which we shall call nodal centers, consists of cities that exist principally to provide consumer and business services to outlying areas or hinterlands. Cities which comprise this category are centers for shopping, wholesale, transportation, and banking activities.

Such a city may be relatively small, serving the needs of a limited area, or it may be medium-sized or large, serving not only an outlying area, but also the special needs of smaller cities within an entire region or beyond. New York is a regional center, but it also provides services for cities throughout the nation and the world. Like most large nodal centers it is also an important manufacturing city, but this may be regarded as a secondary function.

The second category consists of cities which primarily specialize in producing and exporting goods or some relatively restricted type of service. In this category we include manufacturing centers, resort centers, and cities which serve as the base for military installations or large educational or medical institutions.

In addition, there are a number of cities which are not strongly differentiated. In general, these provide some services to adjacent areas and are also specialized to some degree in manufacturing, or as educational, medical, recreation or government centers.

There are 66 cities which stand out fairly clearly as nodal centers in that they are relatively highly structured (i.e., have relatively high percentages of total employment) in a majority of the business service categories. Six of these are found among the 13 largest cities of the nation (SMSA's with more than 1.6 million population); another 30 are found among the 114 medium-sized cities (SMSA's with more than 200,000, but less than 1.6 million population). The remaining 30 belong to the smaller city category.

The rates of growth of these nodal centers are influenced by the growth within their regions, but their growth is typically faster than the regional growth rate. Moreover, as shown in Table 2, their growth rates are higher than those

of manufacturing centers, which are somewhat below the
average of other specialized cities.

Considering these nodal cities by size, we find that the
medium-sized cities, have grown on the average more rapidly than either the large or small cities (Table 2). These
medium-sized nodal cities are found largely in the South

Table 2. Average Percentage Increase in Employment, and
Regional Growth Indexes, by Type of City, 1950–60

	Net Employment Increase, 1950–60	
Type of City	Percentage increase	Regional growth index
New York City	11.6	1.02
Nodal cities (incl. NYC)	28.0	1.60
Large nodal cities	12.3	n.a.
Medium nodal cities	26.0	
Small nodal cities	18.0	
Manufacturing cities	15.8	.36
Cities strongly associated with government employment	36.0	n.a.
Medical and educational centers	31.8	n.a.
Recreational centers		
Nonspecialized cities	23.8	n.a.

and West and are immediately recognized as important regional centers (Table 3). Among the 8 largest medium
cities (with population ranging from 800,000 to 1.6 million), 6 sustained employment increases from 1950 to 1960
of more than 30 percent.

In the large nodal cities, where employment increases
were lower, job destruction to job creation rates, as might
be expected, were much higher. The job destruction to crea-

tion ratios are particularly interesting since they relate the employment decreases (in those industry classifications in which jobs declined) from 1950 to 1960 to the employment increases (in those industry classifications in which jobs increased) during the same period. The story they tell is that the large cities faced greater problems of manpower adjustment. Overall job opportunities opening up were relatively less than in the faster growing medium-sized cities, and at the same time sizable numbers of traditional jobs were vanishing from the scene.

Further light is shed on differences in the character of development in the large and medium nodal cities when we examine the increases in jobs within the business service classification (which includes transportation, communications, wholesale, finance, insurance, and real estate enterprises, and business and repair services). Job increases in this category contributed as large a share of additional jobs in the fast-growing medium-sized nodal cities as in the more slowly growing large-sized cities.

If we consider medium cities, such as Atlanta, Miami, Houston, and Denver, where employment growth was at least twice that of New York City during the 1950s, we see that the share of job additions contributed by business services is typically somewhat above the average of the large nodal centers. In other words, the medium-sized cities were growing much faster in business service employment and were taking on an increasing share of these functions.

It is noteworthy, however, that New York City had the largest share of job increases accounted for by business services of any of the large cities. If we were to examine the New York City data at closer range, we would find that

Table 3. Employment Increase in Percent, Job Decrease to Job Increase Ratios, and Selected Other Measures, in Nodal Cities, 1950–60 [a]

	Employment Increase Percent	Ratio: Job Decreases to Increases [b]	Percentage of Increase Accounted for by Services [c]		
			Business	Consumer	Retail
OVER 1.6 MILLION					
Boston	12.0	.34	10.2	25.5	.0
Newark	12.0	.28	17.1	23.4	2.2
New York	11.6	.26	19.1	25.0	.0
Chicago	12.6	.23	18.2	23.8	3.3
San Francisco	22.0	.10	18.2	31.7	3.6
Los Angeles	47.7	.01	16.5	22.3	6.5
Median	12.3	.24	17.3	24.6	3.2
800,001 TO 1.6 MILLION					
Paterson	27.21	.18	18.7	27.1	10.4
Minneapolis	21.68	.07	16.2	30.8	3.8
Kansas City	21.62	.10	16.2	23.4	2.9
Atlanta	35.0	.01	25.3	26.7	9.4
Miami	81.7	.00	22.6	34.8	11.7
New Orleans	19.0	.15	14.3	28.2	5.9
Dallas	40.8	.07	22.6	26.4	8.2
Houston	41.9	.04	20.2	34.2	12.0
Denver	49.7	.02	17.9	33.3	11.2
Seattle	29.6	.09	14.0	27.2	4.9
Portland, Ore.	13.9	.17	17.4	31.1	2.3
Median	29.6	.07	17.9	28.2	9.4
400,001 TO 800,000					
Omaha	20.7	.10	11.9	29.5	4.0

Richmond	18.5	.14	15.6	29.6	6.7
Jacksonville	43.0	.06	20.7	24.0	9.4
Memphis	15.7	.12	18.3	30.1	5.2
Nashville	19.2	.13	19.8	32.0	6.6
Tampa	75.3	.06	17.5	37.2	17.2
Oklahoma City	28.8	.05	14.2	30.1	8.5
Tulsa	25.8	.06	22.0	28.1	8.2
Fort Worth	23.2	.03	13.6	29.8	9.7
Phoenix	113.9	.00	16.8	32.3	13.4
Salt Lake City	44.8	.02	15.5	35.3	11.4
Median	25.8	.06	16.8	30.1	8.5
200,001 TO 400,000					
Fort Wayne	17.4	.22	25.0	37.3	12.5
Des Moines	13.4	.22	26.0	27.3	1.9
Charlotte	26.2	.11	23.4	27.0	8.7
Orlando	120.8	.01	12.5	30.4	13.3
Little Rock	23.5	.11	12.2	26.6	4.2
Corpus Christi	22.1	.12	13.2	40.3	13.2
Spokane	20.3	.12	13.9	41.7	6.2
Fresno	33.1	.02	18.7	44.2	15.8
Median	22.8	.12	16.3	35.3	10.6

a Based on SMSA data.

b Job decreases are total decreases in employment in these nonagricultural industrial classifications which showed declines from 1950 to 1960. Job increases are total increases in employment in nonagricultural industrial classifications which showed increases.

c Business services include transportation, communication, wholesale, FIRE (financial, insurance, real estate), and business and repair services. Consumer services include sales, hotel and other personal services; entertainment and recreation, private household; medical, educational, and other professional services.

Source: U.S. Census of Population, 1950 and 1960.

shares of job increases were especially high in the important finance, insurance, real estate, and the business and repair service categories.

A final observation is that the share of job increases accounted for by consumer services was somewhat smaller in the large cities. The implication is that these sources of growth have become less available to the large, well-developed metropolises than to the medium-sized cities. (This in turn partially accounts for the slower overall growth of the largest centers.) The difference is particularly striking in retailing. In the large cities, retailing accounted for an average of 3 percent of job increases (in New York City, there were no increases), while in the medium-sized cities it accounted for 9 percent.

Growth and Maturity in a City's Economy

In assessing the problem of maintaining vitality in the New York economy, it is useful to set forth briefly some of the processes of employment expansion in a growing city. This sketch does not go into the determinants of location of basic industries nor does it inquire into the question of how cities are started or developed in their early stages. Rather, it confines itself to the subject of how employment changes are amplified, and why growth, once under way, may feed upon itself until certain constraints develop.

PROCESSES OF GROWTH. There are a variety of ways in which any stimulus to growth is amplified and by which a city's growth feeds upon itself over time. Perhaps the most obvious is the employment "multiplier" effect arising out of local responding consumer incomes. When a new firm locates in a city, new persons are hired. Incomes are received by these new employees as well as by managers, owners, and those who collect rents and interest on loans. These persons in turn spend a portion of their incomes within the city with the result that there are still further increases in employment in retail stores, laundries, beauty shops, and other service firms. Moreover, there is an increased demand for governmental and institutional services such as education and hospitalization. This increased demand also tends to increase employment, for all of these additional employees spend a portion of their incomes locally, which results in further (but smaller) increases in the demand for resources with accompanying generation of still further increments of income. The entire process when fully traced out is the familiar employment multiplier of economic theory applied to the city's economy.

Moreover, as the city grows, additional housing and other fixed facilities such as roads and public buildings are required. If this demand for new structures is no greater than that which existed in previous periods, it merely provides employment for the existing construction trades. But if the growth rate has been accelerated (if it is higher than that which existed in the past), employment in the construction trades must be increased.

Amplification of employment demand may come by several other routes as well. One route is a process of import substitution. We have noted that consumers spend only a portion of their incomes locally. In smaller towns and cities local consumption spending may be severely limited by a lack of goods and services. With growth, however, the market which the city comprises increases in size, and it becomes increasingly feasible for firms to establish themselves to supply consumer needs. In short, size-of-the-market thresholds are passed. Retail and consumer service firms come into being, and the city finds a new source of growth in providing for a larger share of its own needs.

The same holds true for the requirements of businesses. Firms in small cities must import almost all of their supplies and services. When the city grows it offers a larger market for supplying firms. At some point it becomes profitable for firms engaged in the production of producer services to locate within the city itself.

Another route involves improvements in the city as a buyer's market for labor and other business inputs. As the city grows, it becomes increasingly attractive as a place for new firms to locate, not merely because it offers a larger market for the sale of goods and services but also because it provides a better market for the purchase of resources which a firm requires. In addition, large cities provide a labor market with a greater variety of skills and a wider range of experience than is available in small cities.

The advantage of large cities extends, however, beyond the effect of improved markets. We have seen that as the city develops it becomes feasible for new firms to supply the needs of local businesses. If the market continues to grow, a greater variety of firms locate within the city, offering ever more specialized services to businesses and institutions. This itself is significant for a continuation of the growth process. New firms may now locate because needed resources can be readily assembled. Thus, in a well-developed urban center, loans are easier to arrange, and accounting, legal, advertising, data processing, and consulting services are found readily at hand. The new firm coming into the city may "contract-out" various business functions such as data processing, advertising, specialized art work, engineering staff work, and even manufacturing, and thus eliminate a heavy burden of overhead expenses.

The well-developed city offers a variety of amenities which increase its attractiveness as a place to locate. Thus the presence of specialized hospital, educational, and cultural facilities makes it easier to recruit professional and managerial talent, adding significantly to the attractiveness of the city as a place to do business.

FACTORS DISCOURAGING GROWTH. As cities become larger, there are factors which limit further growth. In the first place, there are diseconomies. Congestion makes it more expensive to carry both people and goods back and forth. Rent costs rise and, for a variety of reasons, so do wages. Moreover, as certain amenities are available only in the big cities, so are inconveniences. The unpleasantness associated with air pollution and commuting is a negative factor in recruiting personnel from distant points.

Diseconomies and other negative aspects of large city life increasingly become obstacles to the attraction of certain types of firms (especially manufacturing) for which inexpensive space is a major locational determinant. Moreover, as firms grow in size within the city, certain of them find it economical to locate elsewhere. The advantages of proximity to a large market and a variety of business services become outweighed by the need for space and, in some cases, cheaper labor. Thus the large city becomes more and more the scene of a continuous process in which new firms are "spawned" and others depart.

There is another constraint upon the growth of cities which arises out of limitations on the expansion of overhead structures. For example, once extensive retail shopping facilities are established within a city, further autonomous growth of employment does not bring with it the same tendencies for further stimulation of retail employment. (Evidences of this were noted in the first section.) Similarly, once a basic infrastructure of roads, public buildings, and utilities has been created, it need not be increased to meet the needs of further modest increases in population. For example, the volume of new construction contracts in a given year may decline, even though some growth continues within the city. Under such conditions, the industry will cease to be a source of new demand for labor.

The above discussion is abbreviated and is inadequate in several respects. It fails to note, first of all, the extent to which cities which serve the consumer and business needs of adjacent areas or regions are dependent for growth upon the increasing prosperity of the areas which they serve and, second, the extent to which the growth of cities specializing as manufacturing, recreation, government, or educational centers are dependent upon the increasing demand for their goods or services as a source of growth. Moreover, it fails to take account of the fact that many cities encounter insuperable obstacles to growth at an early stage. These obstacles may arise from a number of causes, including an unfavorable location or the fact that a rival city has already forged ahead, with the result that locational attractions for new firms accrue to the rival. The late arrival "misses the boat."

Nevertheless, the discussion does indicate that the large city faces certain limitations to growth arising out of size alone. Increases in population or in number of persons employed must not be taken as a criterion of economic health. The large city's vitality depends largely upon the spawning of new firms to replace those which retire from the scene and upon continuous adaptation to change.

The Law of Comparative Advantage and
the Problem of Urban Specialization

A basic principle of economics is the law of comparative advantage, which states that throughout the economic system, the most productive arrangements (and therefore the arrangements leading to highest per capita income) are those in which individuals and economic organizations specialize in those activities for which they are relatively best endowed. This means that, when labor is relatively abundant and capital scarce, specialization should tend toward labor-intensive goods and services; where natural resources are abundant, activities should specialize in exploiting such resources; where markets are large, production should be market-oriented.

Cities are properly regarded as economic entities which export goods and services to adjacent areas or to regional, national, or international markets. It is therefore fundamental that the economic health of a city requires that it specialize in those activities in which it has a comparative advantage.

In seeking guidelines for an economic policy consistent with the principle of comparative advantage it is important to consider three propositions which relate to specialization and its implications:

1. The division of labor is limited by the extent of the market.

2. Specialization tends to alter the organism which specializes.

3. In a world of change, comparative advantages are continuously being eroded.

Taken together these propositions point out the direction in which New York's best interests lie and suggest the role which government may play in assisting the city to achieve and maintain economic strength and vitality.

THE DIVISION OF LABOR IS LIMITED BY THE EXTENT OF THE MARKET. This proposition is simply Adam Smith's famous dictum which has stood unchallenged for almost two centuries. The proposition readily explains what has taken place in the fast-growing cities of the South, Southwest, and West Coast. As these regions have grown in population and increased their per capita incomes, the increasing size of markets has permitted a development of specialization in medium-sized cities such as Atlanta, Miami, and Dallas and in the large Western cities of Los Angeles and San Francisco. Firms in these cities have found it feasible to render to cities and towns within adjacent regions services which previously could be offered only by the very large metropolitan centers of the East and Middle West.

The national and international markets have been growing as well. Although New York has been replaced by Dallas in rendering certain services to banks in the Southwest and by Atlanta in providing for certain regional advertising needs in the Southeast, it has moved forward on a broad front in providing ever more specialized financial, advertising, technical consulting, and front office services to the national and international economies.

Thus the importance for New York City of Adam Smith's familiar proposition is that the market in the new world economy has become very large indeed. Although New York City can no longer look to rapid growth as a source of prosperity, it can look to increasing specialization in the activities in which its resources make it possible to achieve preeminence.

Such specialization calls for continued leadership in the areas of finance, fashion, commerce, and central office activities. And there is no reason to exclude the possibility of New York's becoming a revitalized manufacturing center. Not only is the market for certain of the new "exotic" industries, such as the production of electronic instrumentation, automation, and data handling equipment, extremely broad and well situated in the city, but there is good evidence that the resources are at hand for such specialization. The common denominator of these new industries is that each requires a high level of engineering skill on the part of its staff, intelligence and literacy on the part of its workers, and makes small demands upon space and transportation facilities.

In a recent interview, the president of a rapidly growing electronics manufacturing corporation located in the New York metropolitan area pointed out to us five locational advantages which New York offers to his industry. First of all, within the central city the transportation system is excellent and permits ready access to a variety of trained labor. Second, there are distinct advantages accruing as a result of ready access to educational facilities. He has found it possible to make arrangements with technical schools for special training of workers and supervisory personnel, and his company has used the major universities to advance the training of his engineering staff. Third, there is a ready availability of parts. On numerous occasions it had been found that special requirements for electronic parts and equipment could be filled in less than twenty-four hours within the metropolitan area. Fourth, the city is attractive to buyers. He stated that buyers like to come to New York City and that where no other consideration is overriding they select a New York supplier in preference to one located in a less interesting city. Finally, he stated that, for the electronics industry, wage rates in the New York area (especially within the central city) are competitive.

This testimony is by no means unique. For another study we had occasion to interview a number of manufacturers of data processing equipment as well as data processing service bureaus. In general, their opinions substantiated the opinions outlined above, although there was some feeling that wage rates for clerical personnel are higher in the New York area than in competitive locations.

2. SPECIALIZATION TENDS TO ALTER THE ORGANISM WHICH SPECIALIZES. This proposition is widely observed in plant and animal life, but it is important in social organisms as well. In urban economies we see the effect of specialization in the composition of the labor force and in the physical attributes of the city itself. Those cities which are heavily specialized in manufacturing have a small portion of their labor force engaged in consumer and business service activities and a very large proportion in manufacturing. Large sections of the city are given over to manufacturing plants and to housing, and relatively little to shopping centers and such institutions as colleges and hospitals.

The alteration of the composition of human and physical resources is important because it is extremely pervasive and, once effected, it is long lasting. It is characteristic of the free enterprise system that it rarely cleans up after itself. The alterations in work force and physical surroundings which were the result of yesterday's specialization are the city's heritage today. They influence its ability to adjust to new demands in the market place.

In like manner the alterations which today's specialization brings about will be the heritage of the city tomorrow.

3. IN A WORLD OF CHANGE COMPARATIVE ADVANTAGES
ARE CONTINUOUSLY BEING ERODED. Erosion of comparative advantage may come about in several different ways.
Technology may render a strategic source relatively less important. Markets may shift and cause locational advantages
to disappear. Modes of transportation may change, again
eroding advantages to certain locations which were previously favored. Finally, products themselves may rise or decline in their commercial importance.

All changes make adjustment essential. It is here that
cities find themselves bound by the human and physical
characteristics which are the heritage of earlier specialization. For example, in an age of footloose industries and an
emphasis on services and amenities, the industrial cities of
New England, the Great Lakes region, and the Middle Atlantic states are handicapped in attracting new industries or
building themselves as service centers.

When these three propositions are considered together,
we see the challenge and the problems of New York City in
focus. There is a need for new kinds of specialization which
is the result of growing markets. Moreover, older comparative advantages are being eroded (e.g., the loss of competitive advantage in certain types of garment production).
Under these conditions, the city is the victim of its heritage
from the past in terms of land use, the skills of its people,
and the institutional arrangements for replenishing or alter-
ing these skills.

Vigorous as the market system is in effecting change
(and the continuous alteration of the city's skyline attests to
vigor), it cannot guide the sort of changes which must be
made. The role of city government is clearly in focus. It
must provide the chief intelligence in interpreting the needs

for change. It must rightly interpret the degree in which the
city is handicapped by improper use of space, it must ascer-
tain the types of activities which can flourish within the
city's economy and eliminate unnecessary obstacles which
stand in the way of their location, and it must plan for tomorrow in such a way that today's specialization does not
lead to tomorrow's frustration.

The Problem of Unemployment in the Cities

In the years prior to the 1930s, there was very little concern
over the problem of unemployment in the American economy. Orthodox theory held that unemployment, if it occurred at all, was transitory. The marketplace would adjust
supply to demand through changes in wage rates and
through mobility of labor and of capital. It was expected
that wages would decline in areas where there was unemployment and would rise where there were job vacancies.
Unemployed workers were expected to move to those
places where jobs were opening up and firms to locate
where there was an excess of workers.

We now know that the competitive mechanism was aided
enormously by the great need for manpower required
simply to build the young economy. In addition, there were
arrangements which facilitated the adjustment of the supply
to the demand for labor. During periods of cyclical prosperity, workers streamed into the industrial sectors from the
agricultural regions where birth rates were high, and immigrants arrived by the tens and hundreds of thousands from
the depressed areas of Europe. During the much shorter periods of recession and depression, the supply was conveniently reduced.

At the start of the 1930s, America became acutely aware for the first time of the problem of unemployment. In 1932, one man out of four was unemployed. During the entire decade the rate of unemployment within the economy did not fall below 10 percent. Orthodox economics gave way to Keynesian economics, which taught that widespread unemployment was due to a failure of investment to occur on a sufficient scale in a society characterized by a relatively high propensity to save.

The war put an end to unemployment for a time, but in the years that followed the problem returned. The unemployment rate stubbornly remained at a level too high to be socially and politically acceptable. In this post-Keynesian era, there was a new concern which took the form of an emphasis upon the need for growth. The economy, it was observed, showed tendencies toward a slow rate of growth, and, under such conditions, undesirably high employment rates resulted within large segments of the economy.

Only in very recent times has concern shifted from the problem of general unemployment to the problem of specific unemployment, unemployment in limited areas arising out of declines in the demand for labor or the failure of the market to bring about a match between job vacancies and available workers. In part this concern has been directed toward the impact of automation, but it has also found its target in the special problem of unemployment in the cities.

Our interest, of course, is in the latter. The problem is serious indeed, and there is nothing to be gained by denying its magnitude. No estimates of the discrepancy between projected jobs and the available labor supply are published for New York City, but estimates have been prepared by the Department of Commerce for the 25 largest urban complexes (excluding California) for the period 1966–1975. These estimates indicate that even if we were to assume no changes in the number of persons eligible for employment except as a result of natural increases in population (i.e., no immigration), there would be a shortfall of jobs by the end of the period which would amount to almost 10 percent of the work force. There is no evidence that the problem for New York City will be less severe.

The trouble arises from both demand and supply influences. On the demand side, we observe the reduced rate of growth of the large city, and the need for continuous adjustment and refinement of specialization, which is its necessary and appropriate destiny. To complicate the picture there have been changes in both the location and the nature of jobs within the large urban complex. There has been a strong tendency for growth in employment opportunities to be decentralized, with new jobs opening up at a much more rapid rate outside the central city than within. This is particularly true for manufacturing, but it is also true of retail and wholesale trade and even the "bookkeeping" activities of insurance companies, banks, and public utilities. At the same time, the trend toward improved technology has brought with it a new emphasis on white-collar jobs and technical skills. There is less work for the unskilled male and for the young woman with neither skills nor the social graces for office employment.

On the supply side, there are powerful social and economic forces acting to enlarge the number of persons who need or desire employment in the cities. These forces include the displacement of unskilled workers in the rural areas as a result of sharp rises in productivity in agriculture, the increase in racial tension in the deep South, the high

level of "visibility" of the city with its presumed job opportunities (when jobs are available they offer pay scales much
higher than those of rural areas), and its more reliable and
humane welfare provisions. All of these factors have led to
a steady stream of people into the city.

There is also the special character of the natural increase
in the population of the city itself. Since over the years the
middle-income class has tended to migrate to the suburbs,
leaving the city largely to the poorer classes, the flow of persons into the work force as a result of natural increase consists largely of young persons who have been influenced by
attitudes of hopelessness due to the observed inability of
their elders to secure and hold good-paying jobs. Many are
school drop-outs, and many, whether drop-outs or not, are
lacking in the "middle-class" attitudes and manners which
employers require of their white-collar personnel. If there
were very rapid growth within the central city, many answers would be available, but in fact they are not at hand.
Under conditions of labor shortage, skill requirements tend
to be revised downward and racial prejudice tends to be
overcome by the economic necessities of the moment. But
for the central city such growth is not a solution, and in the
face of the problem as it exists we must ask what lessons
economics has to teach.

The first, surely, is that an economy maximizes its welfare when it pursues those activities in which it has the
greatest comparative advantages. If it follows any other
course, it cannot compete in the market place, or it can
compete only under terms which require socially and politically unacceptable reductions in wages or economically unacceptable low returns to capital. Moreover, if the city is
not a vital, ongoing, continuously readjusting organism, it

will decay. The spawning of new firms will cease, and the rate at which old firms die or depart will rise. Any policy other than a policy consistent with the economic health of the city will increase unemployment, not decrease it.

The second lesson is that, although the central city can anticipate relatively little assistance from the forces of growth, there are adjusting processes which, if they can be brought into action over wider geographical areas than the central city and over a longer span than the immediate short run, can go far toward matching people and jobs.

The processes are familiar enough. They include movement of people (both into and out of the city), the educational process (both the training of the young and the retraining of adults), and an improvement in communications between buyers and sellers of labor.

The important question is: To what extent can the private sector be relied upon to bring about the proper functioning of these processes and to what extent must the public sector assume responsibility?

The more closely we examine the roles of each sector, the more clearly we observe the tremendous importance of each: on one hand, it is apparent that New York City's preeminence in commerce, finance, education, and the arts is due in large measure to the highly effective working-out of the processes of the market place. Year after year the city attracts large numbers of the most intelligent and talented young people and professionals in the nation. Moreover, the market place continues to prove itself an extremely sensitive and effective mechanism for matching within the central city persons with given skills and the jobs which require those skills.

But more is required. As we have seen, there are strong

trends working to increase employment opportunities at a faster rate outside of the central city than within. In a recent forecast of job growth within the New York metropolitan region during the period 1965 to 1985, the New York Port Authority has predicted the following percentage gains in employment:

Connecticut sector	37.6
New Jersey sector	36.4
New York sector (including N.Y.C.)	18.2
New York City (including Manhattan)	10.9
Manhattan	6.0

Those differentials in rates of increase in employment indicate clearly that job opportunities must be made available to persons within the city. Barriers of communications and transportation must be overcome. The challenge is great, and bold solutions are demanded. Already some ingenious solutions have been suggested, such as special right-of-way passage for high-speed buses on major highways and "reverse hauls" within the commuter transportation system. A central guiding agency must accept the responsibility. This is a proper function of the public sector.

Moreover, the training function, by long tradition, is a task which in a large measure government must shoulder. The task requires an understanding of the skills and attitudes which are called for in the healthy economy which is visualized. Here again, a mastery is needed of the new trends in the city's industrial composition, and the job requirements which are entailed.

Finally, in an era when the South and West are finding greater favor for the location of enterprises of all kinds and when cities compete for leadership, New York City must continue to attract young men and women of talent and intelligence. There has been ample testimony in recent years that congestion, smog, and the indignities suffered in an antiquated commuter transportation system have rendered the city less attractive as a place to work. Here again the economic health of the city requires public leadership.

2

Technological Change

THE very mention of technological change conjures images of spectacular breakthroughs and revolutionary innovations, usually associated with scientific discovery and mechanical applications. The invention of the steam engine or the cotton gin and, in recent times, the splitting of the atom and the development of the computer, immediately appear as major milestones of technological change. Yet in terms of its impact on the metropolis, technological advance must be viewed in an entirely different framework.

As a major force in shaping a city's history and its future outlook, technological change is a more diffuse and less spectacular process than the breakthrough image suggests. A city's condition and prospects are shaped by advances in such diverse and seemingly unrelated fields as improved fertilizers and farm equipment, jet planes and automatic transmissions for automobiles, better cost accounting, and faster typewriters. Even spectacular innovations do not dictate a revolutionary change in the city's existence. They are diffused, delayed, and modified through the adaptations and adjustments of a countless number of products, users, and consumers.

Without pushing the analogy too far, one is tempted to

observe that the Grand Canyon is not the result of a series of spectacular explosions or volcanic eruptions. It is, rather, the product of a slow change in topography coupled with the equally slow abrasive action of sand and water. In the same sense, technological advances of several centuries in almost every field of human endeavor have combined to give the city its present shape, its current problems, and its future opportunities. This combination of technological changes has largely determined the city's physical characteristics (e.g., space utilization, density, locational features), its employment structure, and its functional specialization. In fact, convincing argument can be made for the claim that structural changes in employment and economic development originate in the *uneven impact of technological change* in different industries. This is the conclusion W. E. G. Salter reaches after examining extensive empirical data in *Productivity and Technical Change*.

A rigorous analysis of the impact of technological change on the metropolis seems to imply a painstaking tracing of literally hundreds of evolutionary advances in as many fields of economic activity. This is an awesome task and well beyond the scope of this chapter.

At the risk of oversimplification, we suggest that technological advances which affect the city can be conveniently viewed as a broad evolutionary stream. Such advances occur in many areas, at different rates and with varying degrees of impact, but they show a surprising consistency of direction when considered from the viewpoint of the city planner and policy maker. It is our further contention that there has been a slow but unmistakable change in the course of technology's stream, a change which has critically affected the very existence of the metropolis. We will argue that the stream of technological innovation has shifted from a force for geographic centralization to one of decentralization and dispersion.

We will then examine the proposition that within the very recent past there is some indication of a new shift in the stream back towards centralization. The importance of the direction of technological change is, quite obviously, an issue of paramount importance to the city planner. It represents the difference between floating with a favorable stream in which external forces propel the city to its desired destination, and the much more demanding effort of moving against the current. We will conclude with an examination of the implications for policy revealed by this conceptual view of the stream of technological development.

Technology as a Force to Centralization

A primary characteristic of the Industrial Revolution and the emergence of the factory system was its marked trend towards centralization of production facilities. The central feature of the factory system was its drawing together of the processes of production under one roof. Further advances in production technology were based primarily on economies of scale. Coupled with the growing adoption of mechanical power, this meant a steady increase in the sizes and capacities of both machinery and plants. The result was a clear trend toward the centralization of the production function.

A second major component of the advances in production technology was increasing specialization and the division of labor. The trend towards specialization applied to both the producing firm and the industrial labor force.

Firms tended to specialize either by process or product line, thereby increasing their interdependence. Machine shops, for example, become totally dependent on foundries, tool manufacturers, and assemblers for their raw materials and equipment. With relatively primitive and expensive transportation facilities, interdependence implied geographical proximity, hence centralization.

The specialization of the labor force, for its part, led to the creation of standardized occupational classifications and bundles of skills. The availability of specialized labor forces in a given geographic area, in turn, made such an area an attractive location for manufacturing facilities, giving further impetus to the trend to centralization.

The stream of advances in manufacturing technology can be traced from its earliest stages well into the early decades of this century. This focal preoccupation in centralized production technology is clearly revealed in the practice and writings of Frederick Taylor from around 1914 to 1923. It also forms the central preoccupation of the "scientific management" and "efficiency experts" movements which followed in Taylor's wake, and persisted well into the 1930s.

At the same time, technological advances in a seemingly far-removed area also contributed to geographic centralization of the population. Advances in farming techniques, equipment, and skills produced astounding increases in the productivity of the agricultural worker. The nation's food demands could be supplied by a constantly declining number of farm workers. And the displaced farmer found his way to the city, setting up a large and continuous centralizing stream in terms of population migration. The process of urbanization of the nation under the impetus of technological advances in both production and agriculture is a familiar theme.

Technological advances in transportation and communications, largely in response to the centralizing urban trend, served to accelerate it further. Public transportation, first in the form of horsecars and trolleys, later subways and buses, facilitated intra-city transportation between home, work place, and shopping areas. The ability to draw on a working population within a greater radius of the work place permitted further growth and centralization of both industrial and commercial operations.

Even the technological advances in as esoteric an area as the art of management provided a stimulus to greater centralization. The efforts of Taylor and his followers in the manufacturing sector have already been referred to. Similar advances in accounting and managerial controls, coupled with improved techniques of organization and planning, permitted the efficient operation of larger and more complex organizations. Plants and offices of a size which would have proved unwieldy for the owner-manager of an earlier era were now well within the capability of a hierarchy of professional managers. Thus a variety of technological advances seemed to combine into a discernible stream favoring the centralization of both economic activity and population living patterns.

Impacts of the Centripetal Forces on the City

The large city which was the focal point of the centralizing technological forces, we have noted, also became their prime beneficiary. Its growth in size, wealth, and employment was the almost inevitable result of the centralizing process. New York City, one of the first established centers, increased and broadened its dominant position. Its early locational advantages in terms of natural port facilities were steadily expanded as the city became the focal point of the railroad network of the region and the major reception center of European immigration. In short, there was a basic congruence between the city's growth and the main flow of technological advance. New York City could grow and retain its economic vitality with comparatively little demand on its policy makers' skills or efforts.

In another sense, New York City became the beneficiary of a happy congruence between two main technological streams. The trend toward the division of labor made it possible (in fact, highly desirable economically) to employ large numbers of unskilled or slightly skilled workers in the manufacturing industries. At the same time, advances in agricultural technology initiated a significant migration of unskilled workers into the city. New York thus became an attractive labor source on the one hand, and, equally important, it could provide a ready source of employment for a large portion of its population with little or no work skills.

This demand for workers benefited not only the displaced farmer, but also the newly arrived immigrant, handicapped by language deficiency and unfamiliarity with the culture. The fact that a large part of the available employment was at the lowest hierarchical and pay levels was not a serious obstacle. The extensive division of labor insured a continuous progression of occupational classifications which could be filled by men with comparatively little additional training from the ranks of lower job holders. In a very real sense, the occupational ladder in industry consisted of closely spaced rungs, and its lowest rung was within easy reach of the totally unskilled worker. Unskilled and semi-skilled manufacturing jobs thus became the "funnel" through which the unemployed were absorbed into the economic structure of the city.

New York's earlier predominance in finance and trade and its prospering manufacturing were mutually supportive. Capital was available for industrial expansion, and the emergence of new firms and the growth of established enterprises provided a growing demand for capital markets. Around both financial and manufacturing activities, an infra-structure of services and supportive activities developed. The entire process was fanned by the operation of the multiplier effect discussed in the preceding chapter.

While this is a somewhat idyllic picture of growth and expansion, it serves to point up the favorable conditions in which New York City found itself when flowing with the tide of technological advance. This happy state of events did not continue indefinitely. For many reasons—some quite independent of the city's growth, many others directly related to it—the mainstream of technological advance gradually shifted. Strong forces for decentralization began to emerge, and the city found itself in a new and far less friendly environment.

Technology as a Force to Decentralization

It is obviously impossible to identify a precise date or "watershed" when the mainstream of technology reverses its course. In the first place the reversal is slow and evolutionary in nature. More importantly, since the "stream," as we have been discussing it, consists of several recognizable

sible, and to distances and locations outside the reach of metropolitan mass transit. This aspect of decentralization applied equally to those employed in the manufacturing, financial, service, or almost any other sector of the economy.

Reliance on personal transportation had several related side-effects. A large firm's demand for space was substantially increased if it was to provide parking space for its employees. This added to the pressure for more elbowroom. In addition, personal transportation substantially increased congestion and traffic problems in central cities. Shopping by out-of-city residents became less convenient, and thus retailing came under the same pressure to decentralize.

Only minor claims can be made for the contribution of agricultural innovations to the trend to decentralization in the cities. It is true that increased farm size and the availability of personal transportation tended to "decentralize" farming in the sense of wider dispersion of farm operations. This, however, had little meaning in terms of the central city. The most direct impact has been the reduced demand for farm land which comes upon the heels of major advances in agricultural productivity. This has served to provide an ample supply of flat, easy-to-develop land for decentralized manufacturing, commercial, and residential use. The large-scale conversion of Long Island potato farm lands is a case in point.

In the last area of technological advances, the management of enterprises, we can note a significant trend towards decentralization. The sheer size of operations, their increased complexity, and their far-flung dispersal virtually forced the need to decentralize the management functions on many large organizations. Managerial units and staffs could no longer be effectively kept in a central location, despite significant advances in communication technology. Coupled with the pressures of necessity, this period also experienced the pressures of a changing philosophy. Growing interest in the individual's satisfaction and motivation in large organizations pointed to the desirability of increased local autonomy and the decentralization of the managerial functions. Many corporations adopted decentralization as an objective in itself, quite apart from the tangible need for its adoption.

Interestingly, it was the continued development of earlier forms of specialization which made subsequent decentralization feasible. The professionalization and concentration of many of the management functions made it possible to separate out and "spin off" a management team along with the operating units which were decentralized. Of particular significance to New York City was the increased capability of organizations to separate out geographically their manufacturing from their office functions, their corporate head offices from operating divisions. More will be said on this in the following section.

The mainstream of technological advance and the major application of such advances thus became a centrifugal force, a force towards decentralization. It is true, of course, that the direction of technological advances is to a large extent determined by the needs and desires of the economic society. It is interesting to note here two factors which tended to guide technology in the period we have been considering. In very general terms it has been stated that American business has gone through a change of emphasis in its most important internal functions. Before the Depression, interest was directed to the *financial* function—the accumu-

lation and manipulation of corporate capital. Considerable
innovation in types of security offerings, debt instruments,
and financing arrangements was the result. In the period between the recovery from the Depression and post-World
War II, emphasis shifted to *production*. Manufacturing
techniques, materials-handling, and productivity received
management's major attention. This was followed by a shift
of emphasis to *sales and marketing*. Managements focused
on their markets, their coverage, and the ability to respond
to their shifting demands. The latter two phases—emphasis
on production and marketing—gave impetus to a series of
technological advances in manufacturing efficiencies and
market-serving improvements. These were the technological trends which provided the pressures towards decentralization we have been considering.

Another important reason for directing the technological
effort toward decentralization was the sheer need imposed
by the constraints which earlier centralization left in its
wake. As noted in the preceding chapter, the structure of
human and physical resources of any location is shaped by
its experience in specialization trends, and shifting trends
do not "clean up after themselves." Yesterday's specialization becomes today's heritage. The heritage left by the
powerful centralization trends in the large city consisted of
serious obstacles to further growth, particularly in the
manufacturing sector. Congestion and density increases
choked off the easy flow of materials and increased the cost
of their transportation. Water and air pollution brought increasing controls and outright banning of so-called noxious
industries in city zoning ordinances. And the growing population exerted strong political pressures to allocate greater
land resources to residential use, often at the expense of
manufacturing.

The earlier trends to centralization in all sectors of the economy created a central city which was not conducive to effective operations under advancing technology. Meyer, Kahn, and Wohl summarize the situation concisely in *The Urban Transportation Problem:* "It can be argued with considerable validity (but at the expense of some oversimplification) that the most serious problems of existing Central Business districts is that they were designed for an outdated set of technological conditions, the most serious single problem being an inadequate separation of truck, private vehicular, and pedestrian traffic." In this context it is not surprising that the general direction of the responses represented by technological advances was one of decentralization.

Impacts of Centrifugal Forces on the City

The impact of the decentralization forces on New York City is well known. They broadly encompass all those sadly familiar issues usually combined under the heading of the city's "problem areas."

Perhaps the most striking result has been the significant loss of manufacturing employment. While manufacturing employment on a national basis failed to show employment growth rates commensurate with growth in output, New York City posted significant declines in employment in this sector. In *Jobs in Transition,* the situation and outlook is summarized: "Since the end of World War II, manufacturing in New York City and the nation has revealed divergent trends. Slight gains in the nation have been accompanied by drops in the city's manufacturing employment. Our forecast for New York City shows a decline of 138,000 manufacturing jobs to be expected between 1960 and 1970." Between

1950 and 1960 the city lost 93,000 manufacturing jobs, while between 1960 and 1964 the loss was 79,000, or a rate of close to 20,000 manufacturing jobs lost per year.

To be sure this depressing loss of employment was more than compensated for by expansions in the service and governmental sectors. Total employment increased by 69,000 between 1950 and 1960, and showed a further increase of 28,000 between 1960 and 1964. In this sense New York fared better under the impacts of decentralization because of technological advances which permitted the retention of central corporate head offices and financial markets in the face of decentralization of production operations. The existence of these head offices, financial institutions, and the complex infrastructure surrounding them, and of the large metropolitan population, permitted the continuation of the city's role as the spawning ground of new enterprises. The process of new firm formation, discussed in the preceding chapter, had become an increasingly important factor in maintaining the city's health in the face of the trend to decentralization.

On the other hand, the loss of manufacturing jobs has serious qualitative aspects which intensify some of the impacts of decentralization. We have already noted the important role manufacturing employment played in the absorption of the unskilled into the labor force, and its function as the first rung on the skill ladder. With the reduction of employment opportunities at this level the capability of the city to absorb the unskilled was reduced. The reduction was due to both the shrinkage of manufacturing employment in total and the additional effect of technological advances which reduced the *relative* number of unskilled workers. Mechanization of many simple manual operations has tended, in recent years, to reduce the proportion of unskilled workers in industry.

The narrowing of the unskilled group which could be absorbed opened up serious imbalances between the city's labor force and the newly created demand for employment. New jobs in clerical, professional, and technical classifications were not filled from the ranks of the city's population of the unskilled and undereducated. Many of the new jobs were filled by commuters, rather than city residents, while unemployment plagued the city's poorer residential areas, already shaped into ghetto-like pockets by the earlier trends to centralization. A circular process was put into motion. Pockets of poverty tend to lower the city's amenities and attractiveness in terms of education, cleanliness, and safety. These tend to drive the middle-class residents out to the suburbs thereby reducing the city's ability to provide the educational and social services needed to combat poverty.

To maintain and expand the city's economic health and vitality under these circumstances becomes a herculean task indeed. The city planner and policy maker must attempt to stem the tide and make headway against the stream created by technology. It is ironic to note that despite the impressive technological advances in every area of human activity, very little technological innovation has been exploited in the cause of the cities' multiple problems. By and large cities have faced the changes wrought by technological change armed only with the primitive tools of earlier technologies.

Consider any city's exploitation of the technological advances we have reviewed in the areas of transportation, construction, pollution control, communications, and management. The backwardness in exploitation of technologi-

cal advances, we believe, is not a result of the cupidity, lack
of interest, or ignorance on the part of city governments.
Rather, it is the result of the lack of institutional mechanisms for exploiting, adapting, and implementing the fruits
of technology to the solution of "public" problems. Suitable
linkages between the profit-making developers and exploit-
ers of technology and its nonprofit user institutions are only
beginning to emerge. In their absence, city governments
facing rapid technological change find themselves in the position of resisting the onslaught of the ballistic missile with
swords and cutlasses.

The recent trend of technological advance thus has posed
a tremendous challenge to the city and its policy makers.
The problems loom large and the demands on ingenuity in
their solution even larger. The picture is not entirely black,
however. We will explore some of the promising recent advances before summarizing the policy implications of this
analysis.

Some Favorable Indications in Technological Change

The most impressive technological advances of the recent
past, perhaps only of the current decade, can be summarized under two headings: the "information explosion" and
the thrust of technology in the sciences. The first describes
the advances in electronic data processing, computers, information handling, and communication networks. The latter refers to the closer integration between scientific exploration in the province of the theoretician and researcher
with the production and physical output of the technician,
application designer, and manufacturer. Much has been

written about both phenomena. Let us, therefore, merely note briefly several manifestations which bear significance for the metropolis.

The rapid proliferation of computer usage in the business sector has converted many offices into "paper-processing factories." * The result has been the opening up of employment opportunities for largely unskilled workers at the bottom of the white-collar occupational ladder. Key punch operating, for example, has been described as a partly blue-collar job. These kinds of jobs can serve as a replacement of the absorption "funnel" into the office, formerly followed by the unskilled laborer in the plant. There is some promise, therefore, of absorbing the hard-to-employ into the work force through this mechanization of the office.

The computer and the recent technological advances in teleprocessing and time-sharing have also strongly reinforced the ability of a business enterprise to retain its head office and management in a centralized location in the face of ever wider decentralization of operations. In many instances, the computer has even persuaded organizations to recentralize their managerial functions. The result indicates an expanding role for corporate head offices and an increase in their size. The ability to transmit, process, and analyze large masses of data, with virtually no delay and little regard for distances involved, permits the centralization of managerial controls in a single corporate location rather than in a hierarchical range of regions and districts. This strand of technological advance at least is now pointing the way to a return to centralization.

* The author has written more extensively on this topic in *Automation in Commercial Banking* (New York, Free Press, 1967) and in "The Anomie of the 'Paper Factory' Worker," *The Columbia Journal of World Business,* May–June, 1967.

The introduction of computers has also generated demands for a whole range of new supportive services. The maintenance and design of hardware, the development of software, and the provision of both technical and operating services to computer users have all opened up fresh spawning grounds for new firm formation. The central city and its existing infrastructure has typically provided the most favorable environment for the emergence of new firms in a supportive function.

In technological applications in science there again appear several indicators which may favor centralization. One major feature of this trend has been the rapid increase of expenditures on research and development. A few key figures will serve to illustrate the impressive growth rates involved. In 1940, annual expenditures on research and development in the United States amounted to $280 million. These rose to a war-time high of $1.8 billion in 1945. In 1949 this figure rose to $3.1 billion, accelerating rapidly to $22 billion in 1965. It is estimated that by 1975 over $40 billion will be spent on research and development. The significance to the cities lies in the fact that a large portion of this research work does *not* require huge land space, is independent of manufacturing and material locations, and is often best exploited in proximity to universities and other academically concentrated communities. A centralization trend in this activity can, therefore, be exploited by the metropolis.

Another feature of science-oriented technology has been the rising importance of the manufacture of relatively small-sized instruments, components, and even machines. A considerable portion of the output of the electronics industry, for example, readily matches this description. The importance here is the shift in the nature of the locational needs of the manufacturer. The pressure for large land areas, single-story structures, and easy flow of bulky materials is reduced. In its place the manufacturer seeks out tools of competent labor and proximity to education and training resources. The point is clearly illustrated in the remarks of the electronics manufacturer quoted in the preceding chapter. In this field of manufacturing, then, the city's comparative advantages are intensified, while its handicaps are minimized.

Finally, the scientific orientation of technology, undoubtedly spurred on by public reaction, has started to include interest in community and environmental problems. Current technological efforts are directed at traffic control and relief of congestion, reduction of air and water pollution, as well as improved techniques of mass education. Such applications of technology are, quite obviously, of crucial importance to the city. Again, we believe, the primary constraint on their rapid development lies in the institutional difficulties associated with meeting the public needs through the mechanism of profit-making business.

Impacts of Emerging Trends on the City

For New York City, the implications of the recent technological advances just reviewed are evident. We will merely check them off in summary form.

Employment opportunities in "semi–blue-collar" and lower-level clerical jobs promise some measure of relief from the imbalance between the skills of the city's hard-to-employ and the demands made by the relatively greater growth in nonmanufacturing employment. If coupled with further elimination of discrimination in hiring and improved training, the newly emerging "paper factories" can be a source of employment for members of the minority groups most severely hurt by the loss of manufacturing jobs.

The reinforcement of the status and size of the corporate head office is so directly related to New York's welfare that it requires no further discussion. The city has long been a corporate head office center, and this function has long been one of the principal underpinnings of its economy. In 1966, 142 of *Fortune*'s list of the top 500 U.S. corporations had headquarters in New York City. If the trend to greater corporate office centralization is to be exploited, New York must make every effort to maintain and enhance its attractions as a desirable location. Otherwise centralized head offices may find it feasible and desirable to move to other locations.

The growth of supporting services and the spawning of new firms has been discussed elsewhere. It need only be noted here that, in data processing, a field of considerable promise has been opened up and that New York City already enjoys an early lead in new firm formation and growth in this sector. A particularly powerful stimulant to the vitality of the myriad services introduced by the new technologies has been the city's highly diversified economic structure. New York's broad base of industrial and commercial specializations has proved to be an extremely fertile ground for the exploitation of technological advances within many specializations and in many directions.

It should be pointed out that, in a more abstract sense, the advances in information handling hold the promise of liberating New York City from its serious handicap of congestion. With the growing importance of information flows, crowded streets and congested loading facilities become less important. In an even more dramatic sense, the developments in the electronic transmission of information reduce the dependence on the physical carrier of that information—the "hard" record which consists of literally tons of paper forms and reports. Consider the impact, for example, of the much-discussed "Checkless Society" on the material-handling functions of just one large city bank which processes an average of one and a half million checks per day. The "Checkless Society" may be remote from reality, but the concept of a flow of information rather than its paper carrier is important. New York City's traffic jams pose no obstacle to the flow of this commodity. This raises the tantalizing vision of New York as a central hub in a national and international network of information flows.

Finally, the expansion of research and development and the growth in science-oriented manufacturing present tempting opportunities for the city. New York's universities and technical education facilities present a powerful base for sophisticated research and production. This base can be expanded by the nation's largest school system on the one hand and the availability of highly specialized skills on the other. The very existence of corporate staff offices in a wide range of industrial classifications implies a sizable population of specialists in almost every phase of economic enterprise. The concentration of technical and academic skills, as we have already noted, can be one of the major attractions for the location of research and production on the frontiers of the new technologies. And, conversely, its entry into new technologies permits the city to take the lead in a field, and reap all the inherent advantages of "already being there" as the field grows and expands.

Technological Change and the Metropolis: Implications for Policy

One fundamental conclusion of our review of technological flows is the rather obvious observation that it is easier to swim with the current than against it. Simple as this conclusion is, it is not uncommon for policy makers, both public and business, to exert great efforts and commit major resources to stem an all but inevitable decline when the same efforts and resources could yield significantly greater payoff in areas of potential growth. The optimum allocation of resources, therefore, demands a clear understanding of the flows and currents of change. Our argument here has been that the most important force which shapes our cities is the stream of technological change. The city planner and policy maker cannot, therefore, perform their functions isolated from technological change broadly defined. Advances in farm machinery, railroad freight loading, and electronic data processing—remote as they may seem—all have relevance to city government.

Let us briefly examine the needs and purposes of technological awareness by city planners before discussing the means by which it can be acquired. We are suggesting that city policy makers must have a working understanding of the directions of technological advances and even some sense of their future probable course. Only thus can policy making abandon its traditional passivity in the face of technological change, and attempt to anticipate it and capitalize on it.

The purpose is twofold. On the aggressive side, it will permit the selection of targets and allocation of priorities to those areas where "swimming with the tide" can yield best results. On the defensive side, policy can be formulated to "clean up the heritage" of obsolete trends. We noted earlier that such cleaning up typically is not performed by the business communities, but is left for public action. The municipal authorities have been extremely slow to initiate such clean ups, primarily because a long delay is involved in perceiving that the heritage of yesterday is obsolete. An understanding of present trends and of the flows in technology will substantially shorten the time between obsolescence and its perception.

There are several critical areas in which city planning and policy can be responsive to technological change. Some of the most obvious can be briefly listed. Allocation of scarce space, in terms of zoning and supportive facilities, is one of the major and most direct tools. Almost equally important are a variety of supportive functions and regulations which a city might extend to encourage and nourish desirable economic activity. The city's huge education and training complex is another area which can be guided and directed to match rather than oppose the technological flow. In political terms, city policy can be instrumental in directing state and federal funds to desirable ends. In this context the very specific target of securing additional technological research, under federally supported programs, for city-based facilities can yield substantial payoffs.

All the above will serve the various independent orga-

nisms which make up the city's economy. In addition the
city can exploit technological advances in its own operations. The advantage of adoption of new technologies by
city government for improved service and efficiency is quite
obvious. Current efforts by city government to make full
use of its computer facilities is a good case in point. Similar
avenues of exploitation of technology exist in other public
institutions under city control. Innovations in educational
technology can be applied in the school system, as well as
medical advances in the city's hospital system. More complicated is the utilization of independent, profit-making enterprises in applying technological advances to more
diffused, environmental public needs. In all these applications, however—whether independent, city-controlled, or
joint ventures—effective policy implies clear awareness of
technological change.

How can such awareness be integrated into city policy
making? One conclusion seems quite clear. It cannot be
done by reliance on the resources of a city's government
alone. The task is too large and specialized. Too many professional skills in too many areas, each with its own complexities, are required. The monitoring and assessment of
technological change must be done in cooperation with the
total resources making up the city's economy, not only those
encompassed by the government sector. This implies the
utilization of the city's business leaders, professionals, and
academicians.

Specific recommendations for achieving such collaboration of city resources cannot be given here. They will, in
any case, probably vary with the particular technology involved. It seems quite clear, though, that a detailed examination of several major technological fields would be

needed to determine their directions and flows and to identify the most suitable institutional mechanism. One example along these lines is represented by the Yavitz and Stanback study, published under the title: *Electronic Data Processing in New York: Lessons in Metropolitan Economics.* Although technological changes were not its sole focus, this study attempted to assess its direction of flow and to draw implications for the city's economic vitality. It is significant that the recommendations emerging from this study placed stress on the need for creating a mechanism for close collaboration between city government and the business and academic sectors. The particular mechanism suggested in this case may or may not prove suitable for collaboration in other fields of technology.

It seems abundantly clear that if technological change is to be viewed as an opportunity rather than a threat to the city's vitality, there must be a considerable acceleration in the interaction and involvement between city government and its business and academic community. The already intricate network of interdependencies between the profit-making, the not-for-profit, and the governmental sectors must be elaborated even further. New and flexible mechanisms need to be established if the city is to respond effectively to the accelerating rate of technological change.

3

Producer Services

THERE is a certain asymmetry in the conventional economic analysis of goods and services. On the one hand, the division of goods into consumer and producer segments is an accepted and valuable tool of analysis which rests on the premise that the factors influencing decisions to spend or not to spend or how much to spend are qualitatively different for consumers and for firms. With regard to services, however, this heuristic distinction has not been made, and as a result the services sector of the economy has not received the intensive analytical treatment that has been accorded the goods sector. Yet in our view, the consumer-producer dichotomy is just as important for services as for the goods portion of our total output.

This classification gap is more surprising since in the United States more people are currently employed in producing services (about 63 percent in 1960) than in goods production—the first such case in the world. I have attempted elsewhere to suggest the reasons for this analytical lapse and to fill the conceptual void resulting from it.*

The consequences of our inadequate grasp of the role of services are potentially more far-reaching for New York

* See my *Manpower and the Growth of Producer Services* (New York, Columbia University Press, 1966).

City than for other cities, since in New York the concentration of workers in services is even greater than it is for the nation—approximately 70 percent in 1960. Therefore, to understand the economy of New York City, to get some insights into its behavior, and, more important, to see where it may be going, we must deepen our knowledge of the services.

Consumer and Producer Services

One important way to analyze output is by potential final purchaser or end-use. For example, apartment buildings, television sets, shoes, food, etc., are tangible goods which are destined to be purchased by the individual consumer. On the other hand, machine tools, drop forges, printing presses, cranes, and the like, are purchased primarily by producers (firms) as aids in the production of whatever it is the firm is turning out. In other words, these goods are intermediate in the production process.

Services can also be classified the same way. To illustrate: barbershops, shoe repair shops, hospitals, and physicians' offices all sell services to consumers for their own use. But management consulting firms, market research firms, public relations firms, investment banks, data processing bureaus, and engineering and architectural firms sell services primarily to other firms (producers). They are intermediate inputs to the production process, and we therefore can term them producer services.

There is one more piece to this classification framework. Producing units in our economy are not all of one stripe—that is, they are not all firms which produce goods or services for a profit. Most of them are, but a surprisingly high

proportion of these firms are in what has been called the not-
for-profit sector—units such as voluntary hospitals, schools,
government agencies, nonprofit research organizations of
various types, social agencies, and so forth. In fact, a very
large proportion of our total labor force is employed in
such nonprofit "enterprises." What is germane here, however, is that nonprofit units are to be found on both sides of
the ledger, that is, they are both producers of goods and services and they are purchasers of goods and services and
must therefore be included in any analysis of our industrial
structure.

This brings us to the core of this chapter. Granted that
the analysis of services has lagged behind that of goods,
within the services sector itself, most of the literature concerns the consumer portion of the total. Very little has been
written about the producer services portion. In part we
hope to overcome that deficit but, more importantly, we wish
to emphasize the unique role that producer services play in
the economic growth of the nation, the region, and the city.
Since producer (as well as consumer) services are produced primarily by people (as opposed to machines), we
must examine the manpower characteristics of the sector
from the dual viewpoints of the types of workers currently
employed in it and the quantity and quality of the workers
who can be employed in it. This is a tall order for a short
essay, so we shall attempt only a broad-brush approach, one
that we hope will bring out the highlights and at the same
time suggest the need for a more thorough probing of the
details.

Producer Services in the New York SMSA

The definition of producer services should now be made explicit: producer services are those services which business firms, nonprofit institutions, and government agencies provide and sell primarily to producers rather than to consumers. In a complex economy like ours, however, it is difficult to match firms with precise definitions—there are many firms which sell their output to more than one type of customer. Finance, insurance, and real estate firms, for example, sell to both producers and consumers. These facts of economic life create difficulties for students of industrial structure, imposing on them the necessity of estimating the proportions of activities to be allocated to one or another category. The present case is no exception, but space limitations do not allow a discussion of the estimating procedures employed—these can be found in the work referred to earlier. Our approach here will be to set out the group of industries and subindustries which we include under the producer services rubric, to show the employment in each, how employment has changed during the 1950–60 decade, and the distribution of the industries within the total segment—in sum, to do for the New York area what we have previously done on a national and on a regional basis.

The basic profile of producer services in the New York SMSA is shown in Table 4. The fractions in parentheses next to the industries represent the proportion of total employment in the industry which we have allocated to producer services. For convenience as well as simplicity we have utilized the same ratios for the New York SMSA as for the United States as a whole. We see first that more than one million workers in the New York SMSA are employed in the producer services segment of the economy. This amount represents roughly 25 percent of the total New York SMSA employment or 1 out of every 4 workers and is about double the national concentration in producer services which, in 1960, was 1 in 8 workers. It may be surprising to learn that the New York economy is so heavily weighted toward producer services. But recognition of this aspect of our industrial structure is of more than passing academic interest. It has, as we shall try to point out, important policy implications.

Table 4.   Employment in Producer Services in the New York Metropolitan Area, 1950 and 1960

Industry	1950	1960	Percent Change
Total, Producer Services	1,005,470	1,084,593	+7.9
Transportation (¾) a	432,729	457,314	+5.7
Communications (¼)	18,202	19,214	+5.6
Utilities and sanitation (½)	30,650	28,643	−6.5
Wholesale trade	228,618	226,640	−.9
Finance, insurance, and real estate (½)	141,366	168,454	+19.2
Advertising	27,294	33,159	+21.5
Legal, engineering and miscellaneous (⅘)	64,888	81,584	+25.7
Government (⅓) b	61,723	69,585	+12.7
Total, All Industries	3,935,464	4,392,875	+11.6
Producer Services as Percent of Total	25.5	24.7	

a Fractions in parentheses indicate proportion of employment allocated to producer services. See text for explanation.

b Federal, state, and local public administration and Armed Forces.

Source: U.S. Census of Population, 1950 and 1960.

The next question is how producer services activities have changed over the 1950–60 decade. There are some important clues here to the problems as well as prospects of the New York economy.

The first item is that total industrial employment in the New York area did not grow as fast as it did nationally— the increases were 11.6 and 15.2 percent respectively over the 1950–60 decade. Of even greater significance is the fact that whereas there was a growth in employment in the producer services segment nationally of 21.3 percent, the growth in the New York area was only 7.9 percent. This lag in growth in a dynamic area of the economy is quite serious, and, if not corrected, will pose a real threat to the future economic growth of the metropolis.

Table 5.   Percent Distribution of Employment in Selected Producer Services, 1950 and 1960

	Total U.S.		Pacific Region		New York SMSA	
	1950	1960	1950	1960	1950	1960
Transportation	25.7	19.0	21.1	15.9	43.0	42.2
Communications	4.1	3.8	4.3	4.0	1.8	1.8
Wholesale trade	25.3	22.9	23.3	19.7	22.7	20.9
Finance, insurance, and real estate	11.2	12.5	11.3	12.2	14.1	15.5
Advertising	1.3	1.2	1.1	1.0	2.7	3.1
Government	25.6	29.7	31.2	37.7	6.1	6.4
All other	6.8	10.9	7.7	9.5	9.6	10.1

Source: U.S. Census of Population, 1950 and 1960.

We can perhaps obtain a better understanding of the producer services segment by looking at its component parts. In Table 5 the "mix" of producer services in the United States as a whole, in the fast-growing Pacific region, and in the New York area is shown for 1950 and 1960. Two dis-

proportions are immediately evident: the greater employment concentration in the transportation field in New York
relative to the United States and the Pacific Region, and the
extremely low concentration of employment in government
in New York relative to the other two areas. Furthermore,
while there were sizable decreases in transportation employment in the other two regions over the decade, in New
York City the decrease was less than 1 percentage point—
constant for all practical purposes. The same phenomenon,
albeit in reverse, is seen with respect to government employment. There were increases of 4.1 and 6.5 percentage
points in the other two areas but a virtual constancy in New
York. This disproportion goes far to explain the lag noted
above in producer services employment in our area. On a
national basis, employment in transportation actually decreased between 1950 and 1960, and employment in government registered a very large increase (45.6 percent) in
the same period. Economic policies which are designed directly or indirectly to increase government employment
would appear to be warranted for the New York SMSA.

It is useful to compare the producer services employment
mix in a region of relatively rapid economic growth—the
Pacific—with New York. We find in the former case a relatively greater concentration of employment in communications and, as has already been pointed out, in government.
As one would expect, New York has somewhat higher concentrations in the financial and advertising areas.

There are, however, a number of encouraging signs in
some of the smaller producer services subgroups which are
not shown in the data presented so far. Some of these are
listed in Table 6.

Table 6. Growth of Selected Producer Services in the New York SMSA, 1958 and 1963

Activity	Number of Establishments with Payrolls		Percent Change	Paid Employees		Percent Change
	1958	1963		1958	1963	
Services to dwellings and other buildings	852	957	+12.3	18,628	26,550	+42.5
Business and management consulting firms	1,163	1,477	+27.0	13,235	17,493	+32.2
Detective agencies (protective)	183	201	+ 9.8	7,285	10,252	+40.7
Equipment rental	240	359	+49.6	1,657	3,105	+87.4
Photofinishing labs	178	216	+21.3	2,789	3,372	+20.9
Interior design	160	263	+64.4	631	1,004	+59.1
Motion picture production and distribution	685	845	+23.4	13,233	15,032	+13.6

Source: U.S. Census of Business, 1958 and 1963.

The first point with respect to these activities is that in each case employment growth in New York City between 1958 and 1963 exceeded that of the United States as a whole (10.3 percent) during that period. Particularly noteworthy is the 42.5 percent increase in employment in services to dwellings or building maintenance, the 32 percent growth in consulting firm employment, and the very large growth in equipment rental both in the number of firms with payrolls (49.6 percent) and in total employees (87.4 percent).

In addition to employment, the other important variable is income. Unfortunately we do not have detailed data on income originating in the producer services segment for the New York SMSA. If, however, we may make deductions from national data to the local level, we may surmise that the percentage of income originating in producer services exceeds the producer service employment concentration in the area. For example, in 1960 about 13 percent of total national employment was in producer services, but as much as 23 percent of total national income originated there. Since, in New York, producer services account for about 25 percent of employment, we can infer that this part of our industrial structure accounts for at least a third of income originating in all industries of the New York SMSA.

Labor Force Characteristics in Producer Services

The prevailing notions with respect to the labor force in the services is that it is relatively low paid, has a high concentration of females, and is heavily weighted toward the sales and personal service occupations. When services are broken open, however, and their dual nature revealed, such generalizations are found to be invalid, especially for the dynamic subgroups of the producer services segment. Concentrating on those activities which are almost wholly producer services—advertising; miscellaneous business services; engineering and architectural services; accounting, auditing, and bookkeeping; and miscellaneous professional services —we find that:

1. Roughly 37 percent of employment in these subgroups consists of professional, technical, and scientific personnel compared with only 11 percent of the total labor force who are at this occupational level and only 17 percent in the consumer services segment.

2. A relatively greater proportion of the employees is in clerical occupations relative to the aggregate—27 and 14 percent respectively.

3. There are relatively lower proportions in the sales, craftsmen, and operative groups (20 percent to 5 percent) and laborers (5 percent to 1 percent) compared with the aggregate.

4. There are higher proportions of male professionals relative to the total—48 to 10 percent.

5. There is a higher proportion of females in the clerical occupations relative to the total—66 to 30 percent.

6. Overall, there is a much lower proportion of females in producer services relative to total employment—18 and 33 percent respectively.

7. There are relatively fewer nonwhite males and females.

8. There are higher than average earnings in these subgroups.

9. There are generally lower unemployment rates.

10. There is an extremely wide spectrum of educational attainment levels.

When we analyze producer services along regional lines we find a very close association between higher than average rates of employment growth and higher than average growth rates in producer services. We have already implied that a low rate of growth in producer services in the New York SMSA over the 1950–60 decade may explain some of the area's problems.

Producer Services and the Future Growth of the New York Metropolitan Area

The thesis of Colin Clark, to the effect that the proportion of the labor force in tertiary (service) industries is an index of economic progress, is widely known. Since in the New York area, 70 percent of the employed are in services (25 percent, as we have shown, in producer services, hence 45 percent in consumer) it would seem that we have grounds for complacency. Yet the contemporary economic picture of the metropolis indicates many problems. Where is the contradiction?

One important clue is the slackening in the rate of growth of producer services. Let us explore this. Economists who are concerned with the rate of growth of the economy emphasize the key role of capital formation (producer goods) and assign to consumer goods a more dependent role. With respect to services, the key role analogously should be assigned to the producer and not the consumer segments. We are not stating that consumer services are unimportant; we are merely implying that the demand for producer services is more closely associated with the growth and proliferation of firms than is the demand for consumer services. Embodied in what we now consider capital expenditures are many producer services (e.g., engineering and architectural services) and moreover, producer services which are less directly embodied, such as management consulting services, for example, also constitute a form of capital investment or capital services.

We see, then, that producer services are the more dynamic segment of the services sector and since the services loom so large in the New York economy, it behooves us to look closely at the problems and prospects of producer services if we are to fashion correct economic policies for the metropolis.

Economic Functions of Producer Services

Producer services are the result of the desire of firms to produce their output at lower costs. When management becomes convinced, for example, that the routine maintenance of a plant or office building can be performed at the same or higher quality levels by others at lower cost than is possible internally, this function will be "contracted-out" to a service firm. As more such decisions are made and as external service firms themselves undergo expansion, their own internal operations become more efficient—leading to further cost reductions. Often, the drive to produce an output at lower costs leads to specialization. The firm learns by experience that it may have absolute and relative advantages over other firms if it concentrates on one or a small range of activities. In this case, many of the functions it previously performed "in-house" are contracted-out. The growth of external service firms then is greatly accelerated by the trend towards specialization.

The Census Bureau's Classified Index of Occupations and Industries (1960) yields approximately 540 different types of producer services ranging in function from routine maintenance to complex economic, financial, and industrial consulting. The major function of most producer services, as we have suggested, is cost reduction, but there are also important groups of consulting firms which are less interested in short-run cost reduction techniques than in providing managerial services having to do with the long-run expansion and the direction of firms, whether through internal growth or via mergers, acquisitions, consolidations, and the like. New York as a financial vortex is particularly well endowed with such firms.

Producer services, in sum, thrive on and contribute to industrial growth and complexity in a sort of synergistic relationship. The fact that translating services exist, for instance, may be a stimulus to the development of export-import firms or to the establishment of domestic or foreign trade publications. In turn, the existence of export-import firms provides opportunities for the establishment of translating services. There is another important function of producer services: firms in areas such as research and development, direct mail advertising, specialized legal, financial, or accounting functions, and data processing, to name only a few, provide a great degree of flexibility to industrial concerns which cannot afford to hire full-time and relatively expensive personnel for services that may be required only intermittently.

All of the foregoing factors, in addition to the highly im-

portant one of the availability of a heterogeneous labor supply from which they can draw personnel, militate in favor
of an urban location for producer service firms. Furthermore, there are many kinds of producer services in which
face-to-face contact is indispensable, as in the case of law-
yers and clients, advertising agencies and artists, accoun-
tants and managers, and the like. An urban environment is
almost essential for such firms.

Guides for Policy

Since employment in the services is conventionally considered as marginal and low wage, it is not surprising that so
little attention has been paid to formulating policies in this
area. Most of our national and local economic policies concern goods and not services—e.g., agricultural subsidies
and supports, tariffs, investment credits, and the like. The
one exception that comes to mind is transportation, where
subsidies have a long history. But if the thesis of this chapter is correct—that many producer services activities have
catalytic as well as initiating effects on the growth of firms
—this segment of the services also warrants stimulation.

Paradoxically, it is in the literature on underdeveloped
areas that one reads a great deal about "social overhead
capital" and "infrastructure," i.e., the investment by governmental agencies in activities such as transportation,
communications, public utilities, port and warehouse facilities, undertaken to provide a general stimulus to economic
growth and development. Most of these activities are producer services as we have used the term, and they are
usually provided by governments because of the large
amount of capital required and the relatively long payback

that exists in the quantity and variety of producer services available in the metropolis. Though more difficult to measure, the cost reductions and efficiency increases that may be derived from the proper utilization of producer services are, in all probability, of greater magnitude than those arising from taxes or subsidies.

To sum up, the basic assumption on which this analysis, and the proposals that flow from it, rests is that the demand for labor on the part of firms is dependent on the demand for the firm's output. Second, any study of the demand for output must take account of the economic factors affecting the potential customers for that output, and the consumer-producer dichotomy is fundamental here.

It follows that policies designed to stimulate employment will be effective to the extent that the industrial structure and, particularly, intra- and inter-industry linkages, by means of which employment is generated, are better comprehended. Finally, the relative lag in growth of the producer services segment in the New York area cannot be viewed with equanimity. Appropriate policies aimed at rectifying this deficiency will result not only in increased employment but in further stimuli to economic growth.

4

The Expansion of Health Services

THE health services industry is one of the nation's fastest growing industries. Employment within the industry has increased 60 percent during each decade since 1940 and New York City is its center. The "top-notch New York hospital" and the "famous Park Avenue specialist" are familiar to the entire country.

Medical and health care is one of New York's major industries, although it has not been recognized as such because of its association with charity and service. It has been estimated that between $3.5-$4 billion are spent annually for health services in the city, and that in the last decade and a half (1948 to 1963), over $400 million has been invested in new and improved facilities.

The health services deserve attention as a major industry, as a rapidly growing industry, and as one of immense importance to the city's budget. The largest increases in employment in low-skilled manual and service jobs in the postwar period, both nationally and locally, have been in the health industry. Many of these jobs are filled by Puerto Ricans and Negroes with low educational attainment at a time when these workers are finding it difficult to enter more sophisticated sectors.

This chapter will focus on the health services industry
from a manpower perspective. It will provide an overview
of developments in the industry as a whole, examine New
York City's place in the national industry, and suggest policy alternatives for the city which could expand employment in this industry.

Overview

With over 4 million people engaged in the provision of
health services, the industry ranks as the third largest employer in the country; only agriculture and construction
employ more workers. The hospital, which accounts for 65
percent of health service employment, is the institutional
focus of health care, and the increase in hospital employment has accounted for most of the growth of the industry.

Despite the overriding importance of the physician as the
key purveyor of health service, physicians are a minority of
the field's manpower. For every physician in the United
States, there are at least 5 technical and other professional
hospital workers, and at least a total of 8 hospital workers,
plus another 2 or 3 workers outside the hospital. About half
of all workers are in some aspect of nursing service.

Despite the rapid development of technology and the increase in productivity which have characterized the economy as a whole during the last quarter century, the health
services industry remains labor-intensive. Approximately
70 percent of a hospital's operating budget goes for manpower. Automation and improved technology frequently
result not in a decrease in demand for labor, but in an increase, which reflects a desire for more and better services.

Also contributing to the expansion of demand has been the increased utilization of existing services, the development of new forms of service, and the extension of services to segments of our population which up to now have been short-changed—mainly the poor.

The locus of health service has passed from the physician's office to the hospital. Institutionalization is expected to increase further as out-patient clinics, health care plans, and nursing homes become more prevalent. At the heart of the industry are the large medical centers which provide a wide range of services together with the important functions of teaching and research.

Institutionalization leads to greater division of labor and specialization. Previously complex functions are subdivided into components and workers are trained for specific tasks. This leads to a requirement of a lower average skill level. The process is hastened because income-starved hospitals cannot afford to pay for higher-skilled workers.

Although the skill levels found in health services stretch from the highest to the lowest, and although greatest public concern is manifest about the highest, the majority of workers are at the lower levels. Fully 70 percent of hospital workers have three or fewer years of post–high-school training, including 22 percent who do not even have a high-school diploma. The expansion of the industry has depended and will continue to depend mainly on increasing the number of workers who need relatively small amounts of training to perform their jobs. For example, between 1950 and 1960, the number of physicians increased 18 percent; registered nurses rose 34 percent; practical nurses, who require only one year's training, increased 50 percent;

and aides and orderlies with little or no special training increased 70 percent.

Workers for these expanding occupations, especially
those requiring little skill, are drawn disproportionately
from disadvantaged groups. In 1960, 7 percent of the professional nurses were nonwhite, whereas nonwhites com-
posed 17 percent of the practical nurses and 44 percent of
the female aides.

Between 70 and 80 percent of hospital workers are females, and the higher proportion of females are at the lower
end of the skill distribution. High turnover and a high rate
of withdrawal from the labor force are characteristic of
young female workers. Older female workers tend to have a
more permanent work attachment, but health services are
only beginning to tap this growing labor source.

The industry is unusual in that each occupation has, by
law or custom, a separate training program. Many of the
skills are specific to one field and not readily transferable to
or from other industries. At one time, most hospital workers were trained in the institutions in which they expected to
work; now schools, colleges, and separate training programs are beginning to take over this function and are
standardizing training so that the workers can move among
different health institutions. Technological and organizational changes, coupled with professional pressure, point to
an increase of specialized training in all occupations and
the introduction of formal training for even the lowest-level
jobs.

This might appear to contradict the earlier statement that
expansion is greatest among the less-skilled workers. In
fact, as each occupation requires more training, new occupations emerge at a lower level.

The industry then, is characterized by increasing organization and institutionalization, by heavy manpower requirements, by an expansion of employment at the lower and middle skill levels, by the need for many workers with different skills, and by an increasingly large training structure. The majority of workers, except at the highest level of professionals, are women, and expansion of employment tends to benefit the nonwhite and less-skilled segments of the population.

New York City

Health services and employment are not evenly distributed throughout the country. The more affluent industrialized regions of the Northeast, North Central, and Pacific areas can support more services than other regions. Although routine services are available in all areas within a region, the highest concentration of resources, particularly those which provide high-level and specialized services, is in the urban centers. The dependence of the hinterland on the city is illustrated by the surprisingly low concentration of resources in areas "adjacent to the metropolis," that is, the outer suburbs, which tend to have fewer physicians or hospital beds per capita than the rural areas.

The highest concentration of resources is in the urban areas of industrialized regions. New York, the chief city of the megalopolis, could be expected to surpass all others, and in most respects it does. With only 4 percent of the nation's population, it has 5.5 percent of the beds in short-term general hospitals, 7 percent of the dentists, and 9 percent of the physicians. Its 160 hospitals include 22 complete medical centers.

Perhaps the best indicator of the quality of medicine in New York is the concentration of specialists: 11 percent of the nation's internists and 14 percent of its psychiatrists practice in New York, and 15 percent of the nation's hospital residents come to New York for their specialty training. Boston is the only city which approaches New York in the concentration of medical manpower and facilities, but even Boston is overshadowed by the sheer size of New York's facilities.

New York's importance as a health services center stretches far beyond the metropolitan area. A one day census of short-term patients in general hospitals in New York showed that 10 percent of these patients were from out-of-town. Since one is not likely to travel to New York for routine medical service, it can be assumed that the proportion of out-of-towners among those receiving specialized services is even higher.

New York is important to the nation's health services, and health services are important to New York. There are no data available to indicate the total number of health service workers in New York. Our estimate puts the number at over 210,000, or more than 5.5 percent of the city's labor force. Hospital employment accounts for about 141,000, of whom municipal facilities employ 40,000.

The greatest increases in employment have been in diagnostic and therapeutic services. New York depends on strong laboratory facilities for its hospitals and is the center of commercial laboratory services for the metropolitan area. The city contains 335 clinical medical laboratories, of which 162 are outside of hospitals. These laboratories employ over 5,000 licensed technical personnel plus suppor-

tive and assisting personnel. The over 900 dental laboratories, mostly commercial, employ 3,000 to 4,000 dental
technicians plus supporting personnel. In addition there are
several thousand other therapeutic and diagnostic technicians in the city, exclusive of research personnel who
are not, strictly speaking, part of health service.

The characteristics of the health services industry as a
whole, which we gave earlier—that it is rapidly expanding,
that employment and increases in employment are concentrated at the lower end of the skill spectrum, that a high division of labor and specialization of training prevails—is
applicable to New York. In addition, the structure of
the industry in New York has several distinguishing features.

The higher level of specialization of services requires a
higher specialization of skill. Whereas in the rest of New
York State, two-thirds of the medical laboratory workers
are classified only as general laboratory technicians, in
New York City 50 percent are classified by specialty—
cytotechnology, hematology, serology, etc. A larger amount
of resources must be devoted to separate training programs
for these different types of workers.

The concentration of health service institutions and
health service workers in a small geographical area has important implications. Workers can change jobs with minimal dislocation, and competition between hospitals for
workers, especially those with rare or expensive skills, is in-
tense. (The losers describe it as "cutthroat.") The most obvious competition is between the voluntary and the municipal hospitals. The voluntary hospitals try to stay one step
ahead of the municipal hospitals, and the municipal hos-

pitals try to stay abreast of the voluntary establishments. One voluntary hospital bases its wage policy on being one step ahead of every other hospital in the city.

Concentration makes possible certain economies of scale with respect to training. Formal training programs, especially in educational institutions, can be economic only when there is a constant demand for a large number of workers of a particular type. This condition is fulfilled in New York, and only the reluctance of the educational system to institute a wide range of medical courses holds back the already extensive development of formal institutional training. Even the training structure is centralized. Columbia University and New York University, together with their affiliated medical centers, offer twenty-six programs for seventeen different health occupations. The City University also has an important role in training for health services.

Unionization is widespread in New York. Over half of the hospital workers are under union contract, compared with the national proportion of about 5 percent. A large proportion of union workers are in the municipal hospital system. The unions favorably affect wage rates and benefits for both unionized workers and nonmembers and provide a stimulus for union activity in hospitals throughout the country.

The municipal hospital system is an important part of the New York medical scene. With almost 30 percent of the hospital workers, the system provides a good portion of the total health care provided to New Yorkers. The shortcomings of the municipal hospitals have been publicized in recent years; more will be said about the system later in this chapter.

Policy Alternatives

Many facets of the growth of the health services industry could be explored in detail. But our purpose is more limited: it is to view the growth of the industry from a manpower perspective and to suggest policy alternatives for the city.

Unlike in most industries in the private sector, public policy with regard to health services has a direct and strong influence on growth. Since health services are extremely expensive to provide and are not profit making, increased demand is not sufficient to create the supply. New forms of payment through public and private health insurance, and increased public and private investment in facilities and training, are the key to the development of the industry. The three levels of government—city, state, and federal—own a large number of the hospitals and health facilities; they pay for a large proportion of the services provided; and, through various laws and regulations, they exercise major control over the industry. Furthermore, a large part of the training is supported by government funds. In this connection the most important level of government in New York is the city, which has the most direct control and the most direct responsibility, and through which most of the state and federal moneys are funneled.

The present trends in health service manpower, which we have noted, will continue in New York City as well as in the nation. The city can do more than just keep up with present trends. It can actively support and further the expansion of the industry and thereby serve to keep New York in the forefront of the industry.

NEW ORGANIZATIONAL FORMS. New York has traditionally provided publicly supported medical care to its citizens,
despite the many problems this policy has presented. The
present financial infusion will, it is hoped, increase existing
services by enabling the city to increase facilities and manpower. However, if New York is to continue its role as an
innovator in health care, it must continue to introduce new
services and new organizational forms.

Bellevue's psychiatric ward, at the time of its establishment, was a new form of community medicine. Now, good
mental health care includes out-patient facilities. New facilities in maternal health and child care are also springing up.
New York has three centers of nurse midwifery. Federally
supported child centers are being developed. In addition to
the 23 district health clinics under the Department of
Health, neighborhood and community health centers are
being established, albeit slowly, as federal funds become
available.

Each of these programs is a step forward in the delivery
of health services. They are new organizational forms, they
are providing care in new fields, and they are servicing previously unreached populations. They are also using new
forms of manpower. Rather than depending on the traditional physician-nurse team, the majority of these new programs use manpower with a level of education between that
required of the physician and the nurse. Psychologists, social workers, nurse-midwives, all have specialized training
beyond the baccalaureate. However, neighborhood and
community health centers utilize a variety of workers with
much less formal education, who are drawn largely from
the local population. These workers are given training

which enables them to function as more than just a pair of hands. Thus these centers serve to relieve the pressure on the overcrowded municipal hospitals by providing out-of-hospital care, and, at the same time, provide employment for local residents who might otherwise remain jobless.

OLD ORGANIZATIONAL FORMS. Out-patient facilities are heavily used in the city. In 1965 over 3.5 million visits were made to municipal hospital out-patient clinics, 2.7 million visits to voluntary hospital out-patient facilities, and 2.8 million visits to Health Department and independent clinics. There were also 2.5 million visits to emergency room facilities in public and private hospitals.

The heavy use of out-patient facilities seems to indicate that they are filling a social need. Yet many hospitals consider them at best a necessary evil and at worst an expensive substitute for a visit to a physician's office. It would be wiser for both the municipal and voluntary hospitals to consider out-patient clinics as a necessary and desirable form of care. Out-patient facilities should be more adequately staffed, and clinic hours should be scheduled less during the day and more at night and on weekends when more people are able to come. This would help to decrease the use of the emergency room for non-emergencies, and would make possible the improved utilization of the hospital when the in-patient load is lightest.

In addition to hospital-centered out-patient care, there are several large-scale health care plans, such as HIP and the Teamsters' plan, which offer semi-institutional services, utilizing out-patient centers with private or salaried physicians. New state laws have finally enabled such plans to offer in-patient services at hospitals under their own control. Such health care plans meet a need on the part of the population, as evidenced by their increasing popularity in New York and elsewhere.

THE MUNICIPAL SYSTEM. In past years the activities of the Department of Health and the municipal hospital system were a matter of pride to New Yorkers. Recently, municipal hospitals have provided inadequate care because of poor financing, inadequate planning, and bureaucratic restrictions. The Health Department has also been fighting an uphill battle. It appears, however, that the situation may soon take a turn for the better. The affiliation of voluntary with municipal hospitals, for all its flaws, has increased the manpower resources available to the municipal institutions; the influx of state and federal funds has eased the financial pressure and made new manpower and new organization possible for both the hospitals and the Department of Health. The reorganization of the municipal government now under way gives promise of enhancing the ability of the city to deliver health services to its residents.

As in most large cities, New York's municipal employees are part of a Civil Service system. Civil Service was originally instituted as a means of assuring that workers would be chosen and promoted for their competence, not for their political connections. From the point of view of the city's municipal hospital system, however, Civil Service has a number of drawbacks.

First, it is based on the assumption of a stable job structure and low turnover, with each worker making a "career" of government service through periodic promotions based on proven competence. Hospitals do not fit this model. The effect of Civil Service on an industry with a fast changing job structure, high turnover, and minimal promotion because of rigid qualifying barriers is negative.

Second, the standardization of job titles and wage policies and the difficulty of changing the personnel budget once it is set reduces the flexibility of the individual hospital to hire, assign, and pay their workers as needed.

Third, the centralization of personnel administration interposes several levels between the employee and his employer. Sixteen separate steps are involved in hiring a new worker. It is not unusual for workers to have to wait a month or two between the time they apply for a job and the time they are hired; employees have sometimes had to wait six weeks for their paychecks. The majority of hospital employees have a relatively low income. Despite the better wage level in municipal hospitals, workers cannot afford to wait for their first paycheck. Under these circumstances it is not surprising that municipal hospitals have a chronic personnel shortage.

Affiliation with voluntary hospitals has eased the situation somewhat, since the voluntary hospitals have a freedom of maneuverability denied the municipal institutions. The Department of Hospitals is currently working toward greater decentralization and independence for each hospital. The Civil Service Commission of the city recognizes the need for greater flexibility, but is hamstrung by vested interests, outmoded laws, and the dominance of the state civil service.

THE UNWILLING TOURISTS. Large numbers of out-of-towners come to New York for medical services. As noted before, a census showed that 1 in 10 patients in New York hospitals was an out-of-towner, and the number in vol-

untary hospitals was 1 out of 8. However, many other patients do not need hospital care. They come for medical
consultation, for observation and tests, or for the special
facilities and services available for ambulatory patients.
Some of the institutes or hospitals have social service departments which assist these out-of-hospital patients to find
places to stay or to make arrangements for transportation.
But many others do not, and private physicians are not
usually in a position to assist their patients in these matters.
The difficulties of fending for oneself in a strange city are
well documented; to make arrangements while one is sick is
a double burden.

We do not know how many people come to New York
for medical help. Although many get here without aid,
others turn to community agencies for assistance. For example, the Nassau County chapter of the Red Cross drives
over 400 people a year into New York, mainly Manhattan,
for medical care. The Red Cross, of course, only serves
those who are not physically or financially able to travel on
their own. Several other New York community agencies are
active in such matters, but their efforts are scattered and not
widely publicized. A central agency which could improve
arrangements for patient-visitors and coordinate with community agencies here and in the patients' home areas could
ease their access to facilities in New York City.

PATIENT FLOW. Steps could be taken to increase health
service employment within the city by increasing the number of local residents treated within the city. The city has
traditionally exported a certain percentage of its patients.
If these patients were retained within the city, the cost of
their care would remain approximately the same and the
employment generated would occur within the city. The

two largest categories of institutions involved are mental hospitals, particularly state mental hospitals, and nursing homes, among which proprietary institutions predominate.

Of 85,000 patients in New York State mental hospitals in 1964, 54,000, or 64 percent, were from New York City. But only 14,000 of them, or 25 percent of the New York City patients, were in hospitals located within the five boroughs. An increase in state mental facilities in New York City appears indicated. First, the trend in psychiatric care is away from the large in-patient hospitals toward out-patient facilities or psychiatric units of general care hospitals close to the patient's residence. There are already more than 160 licensed psychiatric clinics in the city, and an increase in their number is foreseen. Second, an increase in state facilities within the city is advisable because the present facilities are difficult to reach for low-income families, and patients in out-of-town facilities are cut off from their families and friends. Third, the vast majority of workers in mental facilities are at the lower end of the skill level and are recruited from the local population. Over 32,000 persons work in state mental hospitals, but only 5,500 of these work in the city. If the patients were kept within the city, over 21,000 New York City residents could be employed to care for them.

Nursing homes and convalescent facilities are increasingly important to health care, and will continue to increase in importance under Medicare. Here, too, New York is losing out. The total number of beds available in southern New York State, excluding those in local government institutions which are available only for local residents, increased by 161 between 1965 and 1966. However, beds in New York City decreased by 727, while those on Long Island and in the northern counties increased by 691 and 217 respectively. Many of these new beds will be filled by New York City residents; the majority of the beds (70 percent) are in private, profit-making institutions, and the employees, once again, are drawn from the local community. Part of the reason for the decrease in beds within the city is salutary—they were of such wretched quality that the Department of Health closed them. New construction of nursing homes will have to conform to the Department's standards within the city as well as to Medicare standards throughout the state, and thus will be of higher quality wherever they are located.

Although space is at a premium in Manhattan, there are available areas in other boroughs. Since the majority of the population live in the other boroughs, it would be good policy to locate nursing homes there.

Efforts to facilitate the construction of nursing homes and mental hospitals would lead to several benefits in addition to the obvious ones of increasing available care and employment. The patients would be closer to their families; nursing homes would be closer to parent hospital and special medical services when required; and homes in Queens, the Bronx, and Staten Island would attract patients from Long Island, Westchester, and New Jersey.

RESEARCH AND PRACTICE. Excellence in medical services rests on constant willingness to experiment with new forms of diagnosis, treatment, care, and organization, and an equal willingness to translate research into practice. The sources of innovation are many. The concentration of medical schools, research units within hospitals, and separate institutes devoted solely to medical research in the city is responsible for the city's preeminence. The facilities are staffed with physicians and scientists and with equally large numbers of technicians and research assistants with education ranging from a high-school diploma to a master's degree.

Strong research facilities are crucial and every effort should be made to supply them with well-trained workers. The importance of New York as a treatment center depends on the quick translation of research into practice, and instituting new forms of treatment and technology requires on-the-job training for new and emerging techniques. This is part of the ongoing cost of medical excellence, a burden that now falls almost entirely on hospitals.

This is as it should be. Although health service training is increasingly a responsibility of educational institutions, and elsewhere in this chapter we urge greater reliance on them, they are unsuited for this type of training. The time required for educational institutions to respond to new demands and to plan and implement new programs usually stretches into several years. The exception is the private trade-school, which, because of its competitive position, must often be a step ahead of the nonprofit structure. However, the cost of equipment, and the lack of access to the hospitals and patients, makes these schools unsuited for this particular type of training. Only when the skills needed have been researched, when the need for the skills has become widespread and stable, and when the job tasks have become standardized and routinized can the hospitals afford to turn the training over to the schools and the schools afford to accept it.

In the meantime, the cost of quick skill acquisition falls

on the hospitals and their patients. The possibility should be examined of finding public or private funds for support of custom-tailored training in new fields.

Concern about the quality of workers in health services is rampant among city and state agencies and professional organizations. These agencies and organizations seek to regulate, certify, or license workers. However, the skills needed for the delivery of medical services do not remain static, and in a city such as New York the change is frequently more rapid than elsewhere. Overregulation can have as deleterious an effect as underregulation. Flexibility and freedom to experiment are needed to protect quality. The institutions providing service should be made responsible for the quality of their own work.

WAGES AND SALARIES. Professional manpower is potentially highly mobile and is attracted by high wages and high quality of facilities. Although low-level workers have a greater tendency to remain in one area, some are also potentially mobile, and large wage differentials as well as good working conditions can attract them to or away from a city.

An examination of published wage rates in health services occupations shows that wages are highest on the West Coast, in Los Angeles and San Francisco. Employment data show these to be the areas of greatest in-mobility. Wages paid professional nurses and allied nursing personnel in New York are close to the wages paid on the West Coast, but New York falls rapidly behind the leaders in the average salaries for the increasingly important allied health professionals—social workers, dietitians, technicians, and therapists. New York is the national headquarters of the nursing profession and is the center of union activity aimed at lower-level hospital workers, but the newer specialties have not had the benefit of either professional militancy or unionization. Technicians, in particular those associated with the medical specialties of radiology and pathology, are not as well organized in New York.

The quality of these second-level personnel frequently determines the desirability of institutions as places of work for the highest level professionals. The nurses and allied health professionals, many of whom are young, single women without ties to the local area, are likely to leave for greener pastures unless their wages are competitive. It should be pointed out that many hospitals, including municipal hospitals, think of their fringe benefits as an attractive inducement. But young women who intend to stop working when they marry and have children are interested not in long-term fringe benefits, but in cash in hand.

THE TRAINING STRUCTURE. Training workers is vitally important to the health services industry; since workers are the "means of production," it is their skills and abilities which determine the output. New York's vast industry requires a vast training structure. Its six medical schools and its large-scale training of internes and residents are proof of its leadership in the realm of physician training. But adequate training for workers in other occupational levels is equally important in determining the quality and quantity of health services.

More of the lower-level than of the professional manpower is drawn from the local population and from graduates of local schools. The city cannot depend on the inmigration of trained workers, and must make opportunities available for training its own population. It should be noted that at present a large percentage of the technical personnel

are foreign-born and foreign-educated. This is partly because technical work does not require fluency in English
and partly because foreigners often lack the more presti-
gious academic degrees required for the higher-paying jobs.
As immigration decreases and the city's population stabi-
lizes, foreign technicians must be replaced with local citizens.

New York's high level of specialization and division of
labor presents certain paradoxes. On the one hand it increases the number of separate types of training programs.
A recent survey found formal training programs for thirty-
four medical occupations in the city. New types of specialization are constantly emerging. Even short training
courses for the lowest-level workers—maids, porters,
nurse's aides, and orderlies—are sometimes sponsored by
hospitals.

On the other hand, the city's high specialization serves to
decrease the relative proportion of workers who need specific training for health services employment. The trend to
greater centralization of administration and the removal of
non-nursing duties from nurses increases the relative numbers of clerks, secretaries, and administrative assistants.
Thus any increase in the quality or quantity of scientific or
clerical training offered in the city's educational institutions
helps to expand the manpower pool that can be drawn on
by the health services industry.

TRAINING NEEDS. The growing importance of non-health
workers does not negate the tremendous need for health service training. The thirty-eight nursing schools in New York
City are only a part of a highly diversified training structure.
But there are weaknesses in that structure.

Perhaps the greatest need is for more nurses. The number of nurses who graduated in the southern New York area increased by 48 percent in the past five years, in contrast to a national increase of only 15.7 percent. The greatest number of graduates (779 in 1966) come from three-year diploma schools based in hospitals. This increase came not through an expansion of the schools, for in fact the number of programs has been decreasing and the number of students admitted has remained almost stable, but through an increase in the number of students who complete their course of study.

Nationally as well as locally, three-year diploma schools have been closing down in favor of four-year baccalaureate and two-year associate degree programs. But these collegiate programs supply only 20 percent of the nation's students of nursing, and have not been opening fast enough to compensate for the loss of the hospital-based programs. The proportion of students graduating from baccalaureate programs has actually decreased in the New York area.

Neither the hospitals, which are overly quick to close the schools, nor the colleges, which are overly slow to open theirs, nor the policy makers, who are urging the changeover, have been sufficiently responsive to the problem of expanding the total supply of new nurses while the change is taking place. The failure of the baccalaureate programs to attract and to retain sufficient numbers of students deserves immediate attention if these programs are to provide leadership cadres. The failure of the hospitals to differentiate in salary or work assignment between nurses with two, or three, or four years' training is also partially responsible for the unsatisfactory response. In addition, every effort should be made to support the hospital-based schools which must continue to provide the majority of nurses.

The situation is less dramatic in the technical fields, which seem less glamorous and which contain fewer workers, but a similar problem prevails. Recent city and state licensure laws have imposed formal educational requirements for X-ray technicians and clinical laboratory technicians. In the past, the bulk of these workers came directly from high schools or from one-year practical courses in private trade schools, although the specialized laboratory workers, as noted above, have always been college-trained. The new laws require two years of formal hospital-based training for X-ray technicians and in general two years of college training for laboratory technicians as a minimum prerequisite for employment, although those working who could prove competence were automatically licensed before the deadline.

The shortage of X-ray technicians is particularly acute. The few schools which were in existence at the time the laws went into effect were not able to expand much beyond their previous enrollment, and only two new schools have opened. The major teaching hospitals, which have the physical resources to support such training, are reluctant to assume the costs of expensive programs when their own budgets are already overburdened. Shortages are reaching the critical point and wages are skyrocketing.

Weaknesses in these two fields undermine the entire state of medical treatment, since diagnosis is increasingly dependent on X-rays and laboratory tests. The laws were designed to strengthen the quality of workers; now steps must be taken to assure the needed quantity.

Funds must be made available to hospitals to enable them to open schools of X-ray technology. The city, as it is already discovering, cannot long continue to depend on the existing work force and out-of-towners. Since the state took the leadership in raising standards, it could reasonably be asked to assume some of the financial burden. Efforts to coordinate the training in hospitals with that in community colleges could also ease the financial burden on hospitals.

Most of the new programs in medical technology are in community colleges. The many private colleges and universities should be encouraged to support health science and technology programs, since the public system cannot and should not be required to do it all. However, since these programs are fairly expensive, some public funds may be required.

There are many technical workers who do not need college training but who require some specialized training. Although hospitals do most of the training for these people, more attention should be paid to public training programs in these special fields. Hospitals in New York use few practical nurses, partly because few are being trained. An expansion of training in vocational high schools and in post–high-school vocational programs could help ease the present shortage. The Manpower Development Training Program and other training structures outside the academic structure have already trained many workers for the health services. Increased support would help to expand programs to include the newer specialities. But a close eye would have to be kept on the changing employment structure to see that suitable jobs are opened for the new graduates.

OCCUPATIONAL MOBILITY. Training and attracting workers is only part of the story. Keeping them is equally important. Turnover rates among health service workers at best average 25 to 30 percent a year; at worst, they can rise to 70 to 80 percent. Part of the explanation is the large numbers of young women and workers with little skill in the field. But much of the blame must be placed on the poor opportunities for advancement, which make it more attractive for many workers to leave than to stay. The difficulties of advancing up the skill and salary ladder are exacerbated in the health service field by the large numbers of laws, regulations, and professional training requirements.

Only recently has the industry begun to realize that its policy of paying low wages and accepting high turnover is unduly expensive. Some steps are now being taken to change this situation. Local 420 of the American Federation of State, County, and Municipal Employees was able to obtain promotion opportunities in its contract with municipal hospitals for nonprofessional workers in dietetics, housekeeping, and nursing. A certain percentage will be trained for supervisory or technical positions. An important part of the contract is the training of nurses' aides to become practical nurses.

At present such efforts are limited primarily to municipal hospitals. And sporadic efforts to raise nurse's aides to practical nurses or practical nurses to registered nurses are not sufficient. The new project within the City University, which will examine formal requirements with an eye to assisting workers to meet or surmount requirements blocking their advance, is a useful first step. Lower-level professional workers in particular are held back by arbitrary educational requirements for promotion.

Federal funds are increasingly available to hospitals which wish to examine their personnel structure and rationalize their policies. More advantage should be taken of them, and more hospitals should be willing to spend their own money on programs which could eventually save considerable money.

Conclusion

This chapter has outlined the structure and development of the health services industry in the nation and in the city; examined the city's industry from a manpower point of view; and suggested policy alternatives to strengthen the industry and help expand employment. Among the major suggestions are:

1. to develop new organizational forms using new forms of manpower to provide service to urban populations.
2. to encourage the use of, and to staff adequately, out-patient facilities.
3. to increase the flexibility of the municipal hospitals with respect to their personnel policies.
4. to support nursing home and mental hospital facility construction which would enable New Yorkers to receive care within the city.
5. to expedite the translation of research findings into practice by providing public and private funds to assist workers in acquiring new and emerging skills.
6. to bring hospital workers' wages, especially those of nurses and technicians, to a level competitive with wages in other leading cities.
7. to increase the training opportunities available in the city for various health service professions and occupations.
8. to increase the opportunities for upward mobility at all levels of the health service structure.

Every area of the country faces difficult problems in coordinating and planning its health services. New York suffers from organizational proliferation. Scores of local agencies, associations, and committees are interested in one or another aspect of health services, and additional scores of national bodies have headquarters in the city. Perhaps fortunately for the industry, few have any real power or effective control. The efforts of the four major agencies which do—the Associated Hospital Services, the United Hospital Fund, the Health and Hospitals Planning Council, and the Health Services Administration of the city government—are mainly focused on the provision of facilities and services. Each can and does take some responsibility for manpower, the AHS through its approval or disapproval of the quality and cost of services for payment through Blue Cross and Medicare; the Health and Hospitals Planning Council through its state-granted powers of review over construction or extension of services; the UHF through its research and informational activities; and the Health Services Administration through its staffing of the city hospitals and health facilities and its concern with services to the citizen.

But on the whole, little attention has been paid to formulating or implementing a coherent health manpower policy. There has also been insufficient coordination in the manpower area among the four principal groups and between them and the educational structure. In part this is because these agencies have not been able to expand rapidly enough to get ahead of the constantly increasing demands being made on them; in part it is because of the lack of data on which to base manpower policy.

These defects can and should be remedied. The most

urgent need is to collect basic data on the city's health service workers—how many there are, of what kind, and where. The scattered pieces of information available should be centralized, and the additional data collected. Only thus could an overall view be obtained.

Such planning requires knowledge of the dynamics of the manpower situation. Research is required on the sources of supply, means of skill acquisition, and the geographic and occupational mobility of workers. Only with such information in hand will it be possible to formulate good policies and implement sensible and productive programs.

Part Two

Manpower Problems

movements, though the details of these movements are only imprecisely known and include puzzling patterns. Thus, nonwhites who leave New York (typically to move to other metropolitan centers) are apparently better educated than either in-migrants or nonmigrants, while in-migrants tend to be slightly better situated in this regard, and therefore in regard to the demand for labor, than the more stable non-migrant population. There is little doubt, however, that both of these groups suffer considerably in the job market compared to whites, particularly when the demand for labor "loosens" as a result of straitened economic conditions.

Some of the solutions seem to be obvious, however difficult they might be to implement. Thus, massive efforts to upgrade the educational achievements of the disadvantaged should be undertaken. These efforts, according to a familiar argument, would have salutary side benefits in that they would also correct occupationally relevant personal "defects" (in manner, speech, attitudes, and morality) remediable by the middle-class commitments to which schooling leads.

The fact that certain forces have generated a need for better-educated workers in some occupations in New York does not support sweeping generalizations about education as one of the major panaceas for the solution of urban economic ills. Clearly there are benefits in rigorous controls in certain occupations in which credentials, including educational credentials, can contribute to high performance standards; some of these are discussed in connection with problems and opportunities in the health field in chapter 4. But the notion that most of labor supply should be so treated is an unwarranted extrapolation of the facts regarding relatively few jobs in the city's economy.

Faulty Generalizations from a Limited Truth

The notion that one *can* generalize from the changing requirements of some jobs, especially at the upper reaches of the city's occupational structure, is too often an "article of faith" among planners who see education as a means of urban salvation. The upshot is that the *supply* of labor is conceived to be amenable to substantial manipulation while the *demand* for labor is held to be best influenced by interventions only "at the margins." This seems to be the basis of assumptions that inform prevailing notions about economic policy, in general, and manpower policies in particular.

Thus, public actions at all government levels are often undertaken with the aim of enhancing the confidence of businessmen in the economy. Fiscal, monetary, regulatory, and other arrangements are designed in large part to encourage investment and other business responses prerequisite to economic growth. While policy makers may not "give" the private sector all that is asked, it is no less a part of the "old" economics than the "new" that interventions must be made to prevent the disastrous consequences that accompany the pursuit of laissez-faire principles. Subsidies, stockpiles, depreciation allowance, zoning regulations, fair trade laws, land condemnations, tax "holidays," credit guarantees, and finely balanced antitrust mechanisms are among the instruments of intervention.

The status of business characteristics as "independent

variables," in theory and in fact, is legitimized by time-honored (and we may add, proper) references to the sanctity of private property and by the philosophy that it is among the important functions of government to protect property and the rights of property owners. Typically, this status is taken to be inviolable. With respect to the labor market, private employers constitute a significant component in "demand," and because of their historical, constitutional, and legal position, they stand on the side of the important economic "law of supply and demand" that is held to be least vulnerable to change.

Increasing credence is given the view that the changes in the demand for labor make it imperative to *act* upon the supply of labor unselectively whereas we can only *react,* with appropriate policies, to the demand for labor. Whether we consider textbooks, newspaper editorials, congressional speeches, or the detailed analyses of sundry urban planning commissions, including New York's, we find that the requirements specified by employers are the base around which programs of reform and remedy are designed. Thus, New York's planners have expressed serious doubts about whether educational requirements that go up, especially during periods in which the labor market is loose, are in line with the actual demands jobs make. Yet they proceed to see answers only in correcting the "shortcomings" in the labor force, however much these shortcomings may in fact reflect arbitrary changes in requirements.

Indeed, much has been written and said, in print and on picture tube, about the distressing inadequacies of the unemployed, about the changing character of America's occupational structure, and about job vacancies at the upper reaches of the nation's skill hierarchy. A principal conclusion is that the educational, emotional, social, and even moral shortcomings of those who stand outside the boundaries of the social system, marked by "no vacancy" signs, must be remedied by antipoverty and other programs designed to upgrade the deficient.

Little, however, is said about the relationship (or even relevance!) of such efforts to the fact that the occupational structure is changing or that vacancies are primarily in upper white-collar jobs. Presumably it is not possible to modify the unemployed, for whom there is an alleged shortage of low-skill, "entry" jobs, in such a way that they can jump over large numbers of their employed fellow citizens into higher-level jobs. Nevertheless, supply *must* be altered, and we have a well-financed army of bureaucratic mercenaries fighting a "war against poverty" to prove that our capacity for escalation against personal vices and in pursuit of virtue is unlimited.

Tinkering with Demand, Altering Supply

Our fantasies on this matter—and it is the burden of this chapter to explore them—are puzzling indeed in the face of the realities of America's experience. First it is abundantly clear that it was the institutions (i.e., the component parts of the "demand" for labor) that made the adjustments to supply during World War II, when employers, public and private, adapted their recruiting and training to labor market conditions.

Productivity soared during that period while a wide range of people mastered numberless skills almost entirely regardless of their personal characteristics or previous circumstances. The argument that labor costs went up may or

may not be a function of the performance levels and training difficulties encountered in a "tight" labor market. Unit
productivity figures can be misleading in this connection,
for much labor was employed in industries with "cost-plus"
contract arrangements that may play havoc with incentives
to assess and control expenditures for the numerous "factors
of production."

Thus, one of the important manpower lessons—from the
vantage of both civilian and military sectors—to come out
of that period was that "received doctrine," for all its cer-
tainties, was shot through with errors that made the rapidity
of adjustments on the demand side only appear to be a surprise. The facts of our rapid institutional adjustments in
war-time confirm what may be a law: inadequacies in established theory are proportionate to their authors' previous
certainty.

Second, it is consistent with what psychologists and sociologists can tell us to argue that efforts to alter supply (i.e.,
to change peoples' attitudes, self images, achievements, etc.)
are either enormously time-consuming—some require half a
generation—or impossible, and they are always fraught
with risks.

It is likely, for example, that if the much-maligned attitudes of low-income Americans were changed without new
strategies that could ensure a permanently full employment
economy, we might simply add fuel to the smoldering ha-
treds of the more ambitious and therefore frustrated groups
in our urban ghettoes. And to alter the alleged shortcomings
in the patterns of low-income Negro family "structures"
would require modifications in welfare arrangements that
now contribute to family dissolution. These prospects
would sadden further the critics of the poor, contribute to

complaints that taxes are already eating into entrepreneur-
ial and corporate incentives, and reduce, perhaps substantially and more seriously, those margins of reality that help
guarantee the presence of what Professor Morse characterizes in this volume as the "peripheral labor force."

The popular idea that as a society we have more options
in dealing with the "supply" side (i.e., with the characteristics of the work force) than with demand has been reinforced by social scientists. The findings of economists that
there is an association between income and education, and
of sociologists that "upward social mobility" is a function of
the educational achievements of growing numbers of Americans, are pouring out of university computers programmed
by researchers whose confidence in "laws" of behavior is in
consonance with their infatuation with the laws of large
numbers.

Economists are among those who have sought to establish that there is an increasing demand for people with
more education, while the numbers of jobs for which modest education is sufficient are shrinking. Unfortunately the
studies of "rate-of-return" on investments in education assume that earned income is a valid measure of performance
in jobs where wages are taken to represent "value added" to
an enterprise; these analyses tell us very little about the
"real" educational requirements for the jobs arrayed on a
wage continuum.

The salaries of better-educated people may or may not be
closely related to the actual work they do. A study to be
persuasive on this score must present productivity data isolated *by job* and attributable to the specific worker or crew
performing the job; however, these data are difficult to prepare for complex organizations. The "return on invest-

ment" in education for better-paid personnel is in part a reflection of a self-fulfilling prophecy. The fact that employers pay differential wages to employees is at best equivocal evidence of the differential contributions of employee groups at different job levels. In any event, it is circular reasoning to use wage and salary data in relation to educational achievements that are *also* used for job screening and work assignments, and then to argue that salary data may be used to measure the value of education and the "value added" by employees of differential educational backgrounds.

As far back as World War I, analysts have had considerable difficulty in placing the requirements of jobs and occupations on a continuum on which many presumably relevant personal achievements or characteristics can be placed. Indeed the uniform experience of researchers in and out of government at all levels has been that the variation in traits, aptitudes, and educational achievements of productive Americans in all but the very "highest" and "lowest" occupations (perhaps 25 percent of the work force) is as great *within* as *between* occupations!

As chapter 6 suggests, it is not possible to account for wage differentials among lower-level occupations by reference to an orderly process in which personal virtues—educational achievements included—play a significant part once a worker is "attached" to the labor force. Thus, many of the rungs of organizational ladders are nominal in character; although they are linked to pay differentials, there is no close relationship to a skill hierarchy for which measurable traits are conspicuously relevant.

It is interesting to note, in passing, that employers have raised formal educational requirements in recent years (i.e., during a long period in which the labor market has been "loose") in what is a reversal, in many industries, of earlier managerial ideas about education. The result, inevitably and somewhat regrettably, has gratified liberal intellectuals who look appreciatively upon the new economic benefits accruing to better-educated Americans.

It could be argued that one of the elements of the "consensus" in present-day American politics may be linked to the reduction in the gap between conservatives' and liberals' estimates of the worth of education. The egalitarian impulses of America's liberal community have always made room for intellectual differentiations among individuals, and formal educational achievements, rightly or wrongly, are typically accepted as evidence of just such differences. The practical effect of such attitudes and the consensus they reflect on our expenditures for education will likely include expanded investments in "educational" undertakings whose justification may be the formal certification of those who gain access to them! Community colleges and urban institutes are among the expensive certificating agencies that have already appeared on the social landscape at great cost to taxpayers. The fact that these new "educational" centers have had no clearly demonstrable positive effect on the quality of American education may reasonably be an additional source of concern. In thinking of the host of diploma mills that enjoy public support, one is reminded of the Supreme Court's holding, in the Ginzburg (*Eros* Magazine) case, that pornographic material is "material that looks only to titillation, without any redeeming intellectual or esthetic value."

At the same time, despite a modest democratization process, the brightest youth from the lowest income group has only a modestly better chance of entering college than the least able among the highest group, according to a very sophisticated longitudinal study undertaken by the well-known Project Talent.

It is worth noting, in passing, that the increasingly indiscriminate use of educational requirements gives implicit support to the nefarious logic underlying the bromide that individuals get what they deserve of our society's rewards. The use of educational requirements is justified in part by the notion that, given the opportunity for education in America, the less-educated person has himself to blame for his disabilities in a "rational" job market. Blind acceptance of such a ruggedly individualistic point of view might not be so serious if ghetto dwellers did not riot (while city fathers across the nation wonder "what happened?") in cities with what can charitably be called faulty educational arrangements and horrendous obstacles blocking educational achievement among low-income groups. (The details are well covered in a chapter on "The Hidden Costs of Unemployment," which we helped to draft for the 1966 *Manpower Report of the President*.)

A Closer Look at Educational Requirements

The twin facts of unemployment among less-educated Americans and job vacancies in occupations at the upper levels of the skill hierarchy are regularly linked to the educational achievements of the population.

Economists and public planners agree, however, that when employers specify their educational requirements they do so in a rational fashion, i.e., on the basis of evidence that such achievements will contribute to smooth and productive operations. Indeed, this notion lies at the core of the "theory of the firm," which is an only slightly reduced version of received doctrine with regard to the operations of factors and forces in economic systems.

A closer look at some relevant data, however, shows that reality corresponds sufficiently little with "theory" that some revisions in our thinking about them are in order. While the number of jobs for which people with low educational achievement are "qualified" is shrinking, there is not as great an increase in the number of higher-level jobs (e.g., for college graduates) as might be supposed from the frequency with which higher education is stressed. The big increase is in *middle*-level jobs (for high-school graduates and those with some college). The story with respect to the achievements of the work force is that there is a "shortage" of high-school graduates and a "surplus" of college graduates, especially among experienced female members of the work force. The result is that employers, especially those who can use males and females interchangeably, fill *middle*-level jobs with experienced (older) people and with college graduates. These trends will likely continue and be strengthened to judge from data the writer has examined on "actual" job requirements.

While these findings refer to national developments, they seem to apply to New York City. That they do obtain and that employers do seem to adapt their demands for labor to supply rather than to explicit job needs is strongly suggested by other data.

The National Industrial Conference Board demonstrated for Monroe County, New York (which includes Rochester) that educational requirements for most jobs vary with the academic calendar, and that requirements rise as the end of the school year approaches. The argument is made in defense, by employers and theoreticians, that the increasing educational achievements of the work force make it possible to "upgrade" their labor supply, the "quality" of which is allegedly related to educational achievements. In a survey of employers in the rubber, steel, packaging, textile, and hospital supply industries, only *one* firm processed available personnel data to ensure rationality in their manpower practices (including their use of education as what they repeatedly referred to as a screening device) through research. However, even this one firm did not cross-tabulate data on performance with data on the *educational* background on the employees.

A sustained interview effort uncovered several problem areas of concern to employers (e.g., grievances, absenteeism, turnover, productivity, and health dispensary visits), but no efforts whatever to test the hypothesis that educational achievements might be related to the various elements of "pathology" that disrupt efficiency, productivity, or organizational cohesiveness, despite the fact that most of the firms had raised their educational requirements for a broad range of jobs.

One company, in the packaging industry, claimed that it had maintained modest educational requirements, even in periods of loose labor markets, in the belief that better-educated employees would be alienated in its production jobs. A company representative claimed that while systematic research had not been undertaken, it was satisfied with its experience. A spokesman for a major textile company stated that both the company and a significant number of American Indians whom they had recruited had benefited from a *reduction* of educational requirements for jobs in one of its Southern mills. Again, however, there were no data.

Since educational requirements have been going up, and since no effort has been made to test the validity of raising these requirements, it seemed reasonable to investigate the correlates of educational achievement in the economy in other ways. The following section presents the results of such an investigation. The investigation was extensive rather than intensive, i.e., it considered data on diverse measures of people in a wide range of occupations and in many industries to examine the cumulative weight of the evidence bearing on many dimensions of workers' attitudes and performance.

The design of the investigation was drawn to exploit the diverse character of "available data" as fully as possible; therefore, the relevance of particular materials has to be estimated in accordance with the theoretical status that can be assigned to them. The question asked in connection with these diverse data (on worker performance and attitudes) was the obvious one: Do they support the widespread belief among employers, theoreticians, and public policy makers, that there are more "benefits" than costs in raising educational requirements for particular jobs? The data were elicited from firms, the military services, the federal civil service, and public educational systems. Some of these data were collected from scratch by the researchers, and some were taken or borrowed, as appropriate, from other investigations; in either case, comparisons were made between employees of "relatively" higher and "relatively" lower educational achievement in similar or identical jobs.

Managers, often supported by government leaders and

academicians with interests in employment and manpower problems, have well-developed ideologies about the significance of educational achievement. The argument usually begins with a specification of the needs of a highly developed economy and the assertion that with each increment of education—especially increments associated with the receipt of a certificate, diploma, or degree representing a completed course of study or training—attitudes are better, trainability greater, capacities for adaptation more developed, and prospects for promotability enhanced. Simultaneously, those with lesser education, especially those who "drop out" of a course of study in high school, technical school, or college, are held to be less intelligent, adaptable, self-disciplined, personable, attractive, and articulate. The following findings give little support to these assertions.

In a comparison of white-collar workers in a major insurance company in the Greater New York area, productivity, as measured by the dollar value of policies sold, varied inversely with years of formal education, and the relationship became stronger when experience was taken into systematic account. This suggests that education, as such, will not guarantee that an employer, concerned with the social and psychological intangibles of a customer-client relationship, can assume benefits from screening requirements based on years of education.

The performance of young female white-collar clerical personnel, as gauged by the number of merit salary increases (divided by months of service) in a competing insurance company, was examined. The results reveal that there were no differences in the performance records among these females that could be easily attributed to differentials in their educational achievements. Once again, to "screen" job applicants by educational achievements may in fact distract managerial attention from characteristics that *are* relevant to performance on the job.

Both of these insurance firms are located in the Greater New York area as was a major weekly news magazine, in which the performance of secretarial personnel (among whom there was greater variation in educational achievements) was considered. The magazine hired female college graduates as well as high-school graduates for clerical-secretarial positions and awarded proportionately as many selective merit pay increases to the less- as to the better-educated young women. While the personnel administrator was skeptical of the validity of supervisors' evaluations on the basis of which these salary increases were awarded, these evaluations were the controlling factors in this important personnel area.

The employer's argument that college girls need their degrees to qualify for editorial jobs in the future was not easily tested, although it was not substantiated by the data that were available: most editorial jobs were filled by college graduates who *entered* those positions, and not by former college graduates from the secretarial staff. Under these circumstances only a very few of the college graduates among the secretaries stand any statistical chance of moving into this higher-skilled occupation.

Executives of a well-known chemical company, which provides jobs to many New Yorkers, asserted that the "best" technicians in their research laboratory are those with the highest educational achievements. They asserted that this fully supports the practice of giving greater weight to educational achievements as a screening device than to other personal characteristics.

A statistical analysis of relevant data, including information about the turnover and performance evaluations of these technicians, indicated that employers may deceive themselves in the use of educational requirements for jobs. Thus, turnover was positively associated with educational achievement, and less-educated technicians earned higher performance evaluations than their better-educated peers. The employer was shocked at these results, since he had assumed that the performance characteristics of his employees would confirm the wisdom of his employee selection and screening techniques. A closer look at the "reasons for leaving" given by technicians who had left the company highlights an element in the dynamic processes at work in the manpower area: most of them indicated that they intended to continue their education.

That technicians often have educational achievements in excess of what employers themselves believe to be ideal for effective performance is suggested by a thorough survey of employers made by the New York State Department of Labor in 1964. Thousands of companies reported their *minimum* educational requirements under *ideal* labor market conditions and the *actual* achievements of the technicians in their employ. The resulting tabulations indicated that achievements exceeded not only minimum requirements in almost every industry and for almost every type of technician but even the "ideal" requirements of the employers!

It is worth mentioning in connection with these data that ratios of scientists and engineers to technicians were also computed by this agency, each on the basis of a different assumption, as rough estimates of the "utilization" of scientists and engineers in New York State. These ratios varied unsystematically according to a number of criteria, suggesting that the variations cannot be written off as a simple reflection of the idiosyncratic but "real" conditions facing an employer in making judgments about the utilization of his professional personnel. Rather, they suggest that judgments about the mix of manpower skills are made on the basis of gross estimates and hunches largely uninformed by systematic analysis of enterprises' actual requirements.

Lower- and middle-level employees are not the only ones whose educations may be in excess of job requirements. Nor is the phenomenon to be observed only in New York and urban New Jersey. Thus, in a study of eight different Mississippi plants belonging to a large textile company (trouser manufacturing operations), it was observed that there was a negative association between the formal educational achievements and the productivity of several hundred female operators. In this instance the employees were paid by "piece work": wages were thus perfectly valid measures of their productivity. In another part of the same study it turned out that educational achievement was positively associated with turnover.

The findings in this study are wholly confirmed by another like it centered in four departments of a plant in which other garments are manufactured.

In addition to "performance" data dealing with the productivity, overall adequacy, and turnover of personnel, data on work satisfaction may also be considered. While it is possible to concede that dissatisfaction among workers will contribute to a desirable measure of labor mobility and that therefore some quantity of dissatisfaction is healthy, we cannot gainsay the implications of a dissatisfied work force (or group in the work force) for employers. The funds annually spent by employers to improve employee morale, to perfect personnel programs, and to make managerial personnel more sensitive to the needs of their subordinates strongly suggest that managers are attentive, indeed, to the nasty implications of worker dissatisfaction.

Some of the data examined came from a survey undertaken by Roper Associates of a representative sample of 2,000 blue-collar workers in sixteen industries in all parts of the United States. They show that dissatisfactions among workers in lower-skilled jobs increase as educational achievements increase.

The practice of assigning better-educated workers to lower-skill jobs is an almost inevitable by-product of the increasing educational achievements of young people in general combined with changes in occupational structure and the leveling of skill hierarchies resulting from technological changes in manufacturing. The upshot is not promising as far as the well-being of either employers or employees is concerned. Policies aimed at upgrading the educational achievements of low-income populations ignore not only the reality of the occupational structure which is "bunching" at the middle levels but also the reality of the distress among people who discover in the work place that their educational achievements "overqualify" them for their jobs.

The findings of this researcher are largely corroborated by other investigations of job dissatisfaction in which educational achievements have been taken into systematic account.

Other studies, including studies of mental health, indicate that disparities between the expectations of well-educated people (compared to those of less-educated people in similar jobs) and their occupational achievements may count heavily in the genesis of psychopathology.

Turning the Coin

For a variety of reasons, public employers do not typically enjoy favored positions in the labor market and have not been able to raise their educational requirements nearly as fast as have employers in the "private sector."

The branches of the Armed Forces are a case in point. The pressures on the Armed Forces to make do with "what they get" have obliged them to do systematic studies of their experiences with assigning personnel to technical specialties, and the results tend to support the arguments in this chapter. We can report that educational achievement is not only a poor predictor of performance; indeed it is often a less effective predictor of performance than the general tests used in military classification procedures and, even more often, weaker than tests specifically calculated to screen candidates for training programs.

In addition, we note that while there is an association between the number of promotions and the years of education in a 10 percent sample of the entire federal Civil Service— promotions here taken as a rough index of "on-the-job" adequacies—it is a far from perfect association. In a separate study of the Federal Aviation Agency, an agency that was obliged by the age of jet airplanes and the resulting increase in air travel to make major personnel changes, it was found that large numbers of people with diverse educational backgrounds were promoted and upgraded into jobs which they have performed without violence or prejudice to the high standards of this agency's remarkable work.

An examination of the occupational plans of teachers in several major urban public school systems shows that regardless of sex, "better-educated" teachers (especially at the elementary level) tend to plan more job shifts that would take them out of teaching than did less-educated teachers.

Conclusion

The findings reported in these pages raise serious questions about the value of raising educational requirements for work. They suggest that the use of formal education as a sovereign screening device, for jobs adequately performed in the past by people with lower educational attainments, may result in serious costs in terms of the turnover, dissatisfactions, and performance of better-educated employees. Programs which currently aim to improve the education of individuals aim at the wrong "targets"; programs calculated to reward better-educated people, meanwhile, are likely to miss their target.

Thus, from data on which this report is based, the practice of awarding salary increments to schoolteachers on the basis of credits earned toward higher degrees appears to be creating problems where efforts should be made to reduce them. Elementary schoolteachers who earn these extra credits and degrees apparently feel that their educational achievements accumulate to a (relatively low) point where they are "overtrained" for their jobs; then they aspire to administrative jobs for which they must compete with others supplied by other sources of educational administrators or to jobs outside the educational establishment. At the same time, by tacking teachers' salary increases to studies undertaken, the public subsidizes colleges which, because they are in a sellers' market, make few changes in their often ailing departments and schools of education.

Efforts to keep young people in school seem to be more an artifact of loose labor market conditions than of real entry job requirements. It would probably be more reasonable to upgrade people in the middle- and lower-level positions of the work force by providing educational facilities appropriate to their age, needs, and ambitions than to downgrade these people by raising the job requirements for the higher-level jobs to which they aspire. The pressure then would be reduced on lower-level jobs into which less-qualified workers could move in larger numbers. Apparently only after young people, accustomed to earning and disposing of income, develop middle-class aspirations are they interested in pursuing their educations. Yet we have, typically, inadequate facilities for the formal education of young people in their twenties.

One obvious need is that public officials pay attention to these facts and seek more realistic employment requirements. Such efforts can be fruitfully preceded by the reduction of educational requirements for large numbers of jobs in the public sector, and wide publicity when success follows. Studies of the performance and longevity of better- and less-educated employees in municipal civil service would reflect, one can confidently predict, many of the findings reported above.

Nothing in the foregoing analysis should be construed as suggesting that education is a waste of time. Many jobs, as we stated at the outset, *have* changed, and the need for education undoubtedly grows quite apart from the personal benefits individuals derive from their educations. But it is fundamentally subversive of logic not to see the limits inherent in programs that oversimplify issues and questions. The likelihood of oversimplification is suggested by assessing more specifically the nostrum of raising the educational background of minority groups to facilitate their employability. The fact that nonwhite in-migrants may be better educated than nonmigrants poses special problems for Northern cities, especially since within this population group the educated nonwhites have the greatest tendency to migrate. In addition, Negroes whose circumstances have improved have moved into positions that have been vacated by whites rather than into positions for which white workers compete.

Together, these facts do not indicate that there will be dramatically beneficial consequences for educational programs designed to help the bulk of disadvantaged people over fourteen years of age. Educational expenditures will redound to the advantages of the Armed Forces, to individual mobility of those who actually benefit from education, and to the centers to which the migration-prone, better-educated people move.

Since nonwhites seem to find jobs vacated by whites, investments in the education of *whites* will open opportunities for nonwhites! Such a result, however, reinforces a kind of occupational segregation. It will displease Civil Rights groups and simply help preserve traditional wage differentials among race groups. The need for better-educated whites, meantime, is already limited by the nature of the occupational structure in which middle-level jobs are still expanding.

These points indicate that the most crucial policy issue is

the overall level of employment—that is, demand—and not
the "quality of the work force"—that is, supply. Public policy should take form accordingly and seek to avoid misleading citizens by misplaced emphases.

6

The Prospect for Young Workers

IN American society, a man's work determines his income, his social status, and the level at which he can support his family. Deciding upon an occupation is a complex and often lengthy process, influenced by personal predilection and family connections as well as by the opportunities in the labor market. This chapter will show how the particular features of New York City's industrial and occupational structure influence the prospects not only for employment, but for the more significant task of establishment at work.

Establishment at Work

The concept of establishment at work includes those events commonly described as settling down, whether through successive steps in an orderly career or through a period of trial and error that ends in a permanent position. Establishment takes place when a man is attached to an occupation, an industry, or a specific organization; when his income is sufficient to support himself and his dependents at accepted levels of health and decency; and when he has the security of continued employment and protection against illness and retirement.

By this definition, not all male workers become established, since some become attached to low-wage industries or occupations and others fail to become attached at all. For those who do become established, there are two different processes. In one, individuals move toward occupational attachment, which implies the acquisition of transferable skills and a relatively wide choice in actual employment. In the other, individuals move toward organizational attachment, which implies a position where skills are learned on the job and are unique to the particular organization in which they are acquired.

Organizational attachment is most likely to occur in large industrial units with limited entry and well-developed internal labor markets. Except at the entry level, the labor supply is limited to the closed system of the firm, and wage rates tend not to be tied directly to the market but rather reflect institutional forces. The prototype is the large manufacturing organization, although this kind of labor market also operates in utilities, transportation, and communications.

The decline in occupational mobility and voluntary job-changing among men in the age group of twenty-five to thirty suggests that if establishment is made, it usually occurs by that age. But the process actually begins when individuals leave secondary school. By then, there are three major streams—the drop-outs, the graduates who go on to college, and the graduates who enter the labor market. The plight of drop-outs is well known; they are especially disadvantaged in today's employment scene not only because dropping out has been defined as failure, but also because the economy has little use for the labor of the young and unskilled. The usual age of entry into work has been rising steadily, and jobs for those under eighteen are limited.

Entry workers of even eighteen are not considered desirable employees, and large firms hire very few younger than twenty.

Most male high-school graduates have not acquired well-defined occupational skills. Graduates of vocational schools are seldom considered fully trained by prospective employers, and the majority of graduates of other high schools have usually received no occupational preparation. In so far as formal schooling contributes to specific preparation for work, the trend toward post–high-school training is clear; in this respect, the graduates of two-year technical or occupational programs such as are available at community colleges probably have better immediate prospects than graduates of four-year liberal arts program. The liberal arts drop-out has little advantage over the high-school graduate except that he is a year or two older.

In any case, men with specific occupational preparation have an advantage in the labor market roughly in proportion to the level of their skill. Those without pre-employment training tend to seek organizational posts, and this is as true of the liberal arts college graduate as of the untrained high-school graduate. The strength of the organization and the level of attachment become the determining factors in establishment. Thus, a college graduate may enter the lowest ranks of management in a prosperous and expanding firm and outstrip the university faculty member in income and prerequisites. Similarly, the untrained high-school graduate may find his way into a well-articulated internal labor market and, through his attachment to the firm, acquire skill and move up the promotion ladder of non-managerial workers.

The Search for Work

Most young entry workers begin with only a general notion
of the kind of job they are seeking. Those with specific pre-
employment training, high-school girls with clerical skills,
apprentices, and the graduates of two- or four-year training
programs have a better defined field of operation, but even
they are often unaware of the nuances of difference
among possible sites of employment. Nevertheless, their
training makes it easier to use organized placement services.

For the untrained, the information network on employment opportunity has serious defects. For the most part, it
has negative characteristics—it is not a net and it does not
work. The labor market is not a bourse where standard
units are traded, nor do most job seekers engage in a systematic search. In New York, as elsewhere, most information comes from one's family and circle of acquaintance.
Direct referral of family members may take place somewhat
less frequently than in smaller markets, but the perception
of possibilities is circumscribed by the experiences of the
immediate milieu. The less desirable the young worker on
the basis of conventional criteria, the more important is the
specific help available through the family. The operator of a
gas station may take on an errant nephew who has dropped
out of school at sixteen, who otherwise would be unemployable. A young son may become a helper to a self-employed
father for little or no wages. But by and large, the amount
of help available from one's family is usually in inverse proportion to the need. Negro boys in the ghetto, for example,

seldom have alternate opportunities or personal intervention on their behalf.

Private employment agencies, which do a greater share
of placements in New York than in any other city, are usually not concerned with young men. The public employment service maintains a placement program in cooperation
with schools, but because of the prevailing mode of personal contact, it does not account for a major share of
placements. Newspaper ads are an important source of information, but they tend to be directed toward experienced
personnel in specific occupations, specially trained technical personnel, and a variety of clerical positions.

Through one or more of these sources, a personable
young man with minimal literacy can usually obtain a job;
whether this job, or the next one, will lead to establishment
is, as we shall see, another question. There is now little expectation that young workers will stay on their first jobs. In
fact, the system seems to be organized to preclude early decision. Post–high-school education, military service, and
the dead-end nature of many entry jobs combine to make
the early years at work a period characterized by many job
changes. Depending on the outcome, they can be considered either a useful exploratory period or a time of aimless floundering.

Location and Transportation

As in every large city, location and transportation play a
role in the search for work in New York. Its rapid transit
system, the best in the nation, permits job seekers to consider a large geographic area, but the primary job market

is Manhattan below 60th Street. When vacancies occur in outlying areas of the other boroughs, and particularly in the ring of suburbs, inner-city residents find it difficult to apply. In fact, for many of the coveted jobs in large manufacturing plants, the job seeker often says, "You can't get there from here."

The problem of transportation to outlying jobs has not been exacerbated by the movement of large plants as it has in cities like Chicago and Los Angeles. New York City never had many large units, and although some manufacturing jobs have been lost, the major economic functions of the city have long been in finance and trade. Better transportation would enhance opportunity in blue-collar employment, but it is not as critical an issue as in other metropolitan areas.

Employment Opportunity

What, in fact, are the opportunities for work establishment available to young men? At the upper levels of skill and talent, New York is a mecca for the world, with an influx that has always been at least great enough to meet the demand. But the opulence of the city is not quite skin-deep. Below the very top, wages are relatively low, in part because of the industrial mix of the city. Of a total of 3.6 million jobs in 1965, 2.7 million were in nonmanufacturing, and the only sectors which showed gains in employment over the past two decades were finance, insurance, and real estate; service and miscellaneous; and government.

Women in the Labor Force

One effect of this unique distribution of workers is the disproportionate influence of female job constellations. Women make up about one-third of the city's labor force, a proportion not significantly different from the national average, but because their wage rates are low relative to those of men, the positions they fill tend to depress the wage levels for both sexes. New York has an unusually large number of jobs for male clerical workers, but salaries are significantly lower than for manufacturing jobs which require far less educational achievement.

Just as important as wages is the structure of female employment. Women's jobs are rarely organized according to promotion ladders. Skilled clerical workers—from keypunch operators to legal secretaries—usually learn their skills before their first job. The basic source of skilled clerical workers is from among high-school graduates. A new or an added skill may mean promotion, but skill acquisition typically does not take place on the job. The large number of women operators in the apparel industry *do* learn on the job, but here again, the structure is flat and offers little promotional opportunity.

The work that women do is critical for the economy; those who are heads of households must support themselves and their dependents, and those whose earnings are supplementary may raise the family above the poverty level. But the large mass of women's jobs are organized in such a way that they form a kind of ladies' auxiliary, and in New York, the prevalence of white-collar, nonmanufacturing employment has important consequences for wage levels and promotion patterns.

Size of Firms

A basic feature of the city's economy is the small size of the typical firm. In some industries, which use workers from the same pool, small size is not a deterrent to work establishment. In construction, for example, attachment is typically to the occupation rather than to the firm. But while journeymen are in a protected position, the probability that laborers on the fringes of the industry will become established is always slight.

Jobs at a lower level of skill, for example, longshore and trucking jobs, exhibit some of the same features as construction. Internal labor markets with extensive promotion opportunities are, however, found mainly in utilities, communications, and government. These industries, plus transportation and construction, accounted at most for 25 percent of the city's employment in 1965, and the only one likely to experience significant growth in the future is local government. Furthermore, all of these except government are particularly prone to familial recruitment and have very small percentages of Negro and Puerto Rican workers.

The small size of manufacturing firms presents a particular problem in articulation. Few are capable of providing training adequate for upgrading the available work force. In the plastics industry, for example, a small company may need one highly trained extrusion machine operator, but be unwilling or unable either to pay a high enough wage to attract a man from the external market or to train a man already employed in a less-skilled position. The total demand for such operators is so small that pre-employment training is not a feasible solution. Even apart from such extreme cases, supply and demand are in unstable equilibrium. Blue-collar jobs in small shops are filled, but turnover is high in marginal operations. The problem seems to be that employers desire fully productive workers even in positions for which comparable experience is hard to achieve, while the supply of workers at relatively low wage rates is likely to be untrained. In the terms we have used in this chapter, employers are recruiting men with skills, while workers are seeking positions.

In other cities, where both large and small units operate in the same industry (for example, metalworking in Hartford, Connecticut), big firms may train workers for the whole industry. Such workers may moonlight in small shops or move over entirely, especially when the small shops are in a satellite relationship to the large ones, and the wage differential necessary for hiring away skilled men is facilitated through the routine of subcontracting. There is no such convenient mutuality in New York. Undoubtedly, some of the small specialty manufacturing in the city is highly profitable, but many units are marginal and have no guarantee of a stable supply of workers specifically trained for their operations or even of a stable demand for such workers.

In the apparel and printing and publishing industries, which together account for 60 percent of manufacturing jobs and 11 percent of the city's total employment, firms are small and attachment is more likely to be occupational than organizational. In apparel, as we have pointed out, women operators are the most important single occupational group; in printing, women account for 32 percent of the labor force, mainly in clerical positions and in bookbinding.

Manpower Strategies for Youth

Even this brief sketch of New York City's labor market suggests the difficulties encountered by young men in the process of becoming established at work. At current rates, only about 11 percent of the resident labor force are college graduates, and about one-half have not completed high school. While the proportion of educated individuals in the labor force will increase as older workers retire, the labor force of the city will remain essentially unskilled in the foreseeable future.

The problem of providing opportunity is not a new one; it has been acute since 1958, and since then every conceivable type of program has been tried, at least on a pilot basis. Although many of these efforts have been sporadic and uncoordinated, and in some cases wasteful, two conclusions emerge from the experience. First, no program or combination of programs has come close to dealing with the problem quantitatively, no matter what the qualitative success; and second, no single effort can deal with the whole question.

None of the strategies discussed below will be novel to the informed reader. Most of them have been and will continue to be effective only at the margins, because more basic solutions require major structural changes involving the national allocation of resources. Thus, a long-range plan for massive physical renewal might provide the opportunity for negotiating a permanent expansion of jobs with the building trades unions; higher standards of medical care might provide better-paying jobs in paramedical fields; adequate repair services for the gadget-minded might provide the private sector with an opportunity to expand employment. But all of these approaches, although long on the agenda, have been slow in realization. In the meantime, children grow into young adults who need not only jobs but employment adequate for a stable life in the community.

Improving Worker Quality

The single most popular solution, and the one on which consensus can be reached in almost every quarter, is more and better education. Disagreement remains, however, about how this type of improvement in the labor supply will affect demand. It can be argued that the long-term trend toward higher educational achievement has raised requirements for employment, leaving the less educated at the end of the queue regardless of what the job really demands. If the level is raised even higher, the effect would be increased competition for jobs at the top, and escalation of requirements at the bottom. There is little evidence to suggest that improvement in the supply would materially enhance opportunity. On the contrary, employment in New York City is already weighted in favor of clerical and service jobs that require more education and pay significantly less than blue-collar jobs in manufacturing.

There are excellent reasons to improve the quality and to lengthen the educational experience, but it may be that these are requirements for citizenship and for consumption rather than for raising occupational competence. The proverbial Philadelphia lawyer would have difficulty understanding the terms and conditions of credit arrangements made every day by millions of consumers; actual requirements for most jobs in the economy are really less complex. In any case, there is little evidence that there will be a dramatic change with respect to education. There has already been some improvement in quantity, at the expense, some critics claim, of quality. But even if current experiments develop hitherto neglected potential, the number of disadvantaged persons will not be substantially reduced.

The proponents of occupational training have had ample opportunity to experiment in recent years. In New York City we have had proposals to extend, reform, or abolish the vocational schools; we have seen the expansion of community college courses of study, cooperative education largely in clerical and retail occupations, and special training under a variety of auspices. Here again, some conclusions are warranted. First, the trend toward post–high-school training is unmistakable, largely because of the reluctance of employers to accept either the worker or the training produced by the vocational high schools. The only significant exceptions are young female clericals. Second, at the post–high-school level, the community colleges are an important resource, although we have not adequately provided for the support of students who must forego income to take training at these institutions. Third, all other things being equal, training that is at least partly on the job is far more successful than classroom training alone. It is difficult to expand on-the-job training in the small units characteristic of New York, but sponsorship by unions and trade association can overcome some of the barriers.

Closely related to education and training is the general issue of what to do until the job is available. High school

and college share an important secondary characteristic—
they obviate early labor market participation, and this function becomes more important as the very young grow increasingly employable by reason of their age alone. Despite
all the programs devised as a moral equivalent of school or
work, we have not yet made significant inroads on this
problem. Apart from specific plans, what is most needed in
this respect is a commitment to make the transition to maturity less hectic, less problematical, less aimless. As it is,
the young are more valued in the economy as consumers
than as producers. Far removed from work, particularly its
organizational aspects, young people can hardly be expected to emerge into the labor market with appropriate attitudes or developed skills, either of a technical or an inter-
personal nature. Nor is the prevailing ethos of the school
conducive to the development of the cooperative spirit usually demanded in the workplace. Even in the rarified
heights in science, there is no place for an Arrowsmith
alone with his microscope. The tasks assigned in school may
be called work, but they typically are performed alone and
competitively, in contrast to the complex interdependence
of the laboratory, the shop, or the office.

In recent years the largest experiment in programing for
transition has been the Neighborhood Youth Corps. Apart
from the fact that it has been underfinanced, it has also
lacked adequate ties to the full-time permanent job market.
Participants have been provided with pocket money and
minimal work experience, which by law has been in the
public and nonprofit sectors. Like all such efforts, it is difficult to assess the benefits. One thing, however, is clear: if the
program is valuable as a way to bring young people into
contact with the facts of life of the labor market, it should

be extended in various forms so as to provide experiences for a much larger group.

The aim of such an effort, or series of efforts, should be not to routinize the process of becoming established at work, but to minimize the dysfunctional aspects of floundering. Turnover has costs to the worker as well as to the employer. Even more important are the positive benefits that would accrue—opportunities to explore careers could broaden the area of search rather than constrict it.

Changing the Nature of Demand

While efforts to improve the quality of entry workers and to find more fruitful ways of utilizing the talents and energies of youth should continue, more attention should also be paid both to understanding and to changing the nature of demand. It should be stated that major structural changes are no more likely in this respect than in population mix or in the preparation of workers. It is clear, for example, that manufacturing jobs will continue to decline in the city, and that establishments will not miraculously grow larger. This means that well-paying jobs for non-college men are not automatically going to appear in sufficient numbers, and it implies that new and different efforts should be directed toward rationalizing opportunity in small establishments.

These efforts must proceed along several lines, several of which already exist in embryo. First, since the urge for entrepreneurship is far from dead, particularly among aspiring minorities, and since New York City is predominantly a place of small businesses, more must be done to improve the chances of success for new ventures. The present resources of the Small Business Administration are inadequate to the task, especially in New York where capital requirements are high. Furthermore, the administrative rules are too constricting. One gets the impression that even conservative bankers are willing to take more risks than is the SBA.

Just as important as liberalization of credit is the provision of a variety of management aids, ranging from information on the probable volume of business for a small retail store in a given location to advice on establishing training for a handful of workers in a small shop. In the area of manpower utilization, the New York State Employment Service already provides some help through the Industrial Services Program, which is carried on in conjunction with its occupational analysis function. In its model form, industrial service is designed to provide consultation on problems of manpower recruitment, selection, and utilization, with its major aim the stabilization of the work force. Unfortunately, the program is not developed on a very large scale in New York, and its operation could be improved with respect to scope and morale.

The task is critical and is appropriate to a public agency, since the clientele served is precisely the kind of small enterprise that lacks access either to resident or consultative expertise. The case materials of the Industrial Services Program demonstrate how often problems arise that require reassessment of some current practice. Among these are job redesign, changes in stated requirements for employment, and analysis of worker-supervisor relationships that impede the flow of work. An important aim of such service is to decrease wasteful turnover, on the assumption that organization in the workplace is just as important to stability as the initial match of job and worker. This is even more important for young workers who need special supervisory assistance.

While expansion of this aspect of public employment services is desirable, it can succeed only as its functions are strengthened. At present the agency becomes involved in consultation only when repeated difficulties arise in filling job orders for the same firm. This means that it gets only the hardest problems, which tends to discourage the staff. In order to make a significant contribution to employment and utilization, the activities of the Industrial Services Program would have to be redesigned to furnish consultation on a regular basis rather than in emergencies only.

The Employment Service is faced with the more general challenge of increasing its share of placements, but in the meantime, each special program for training or rehabilitating workers has a so-called job development function, which usually implies beating the bushes for placements. The well-known employers in the city have complained about the frequency with which they are asked by competing agencies to furnish openings, but there has been no effort to canvass the experience of the "job developers" and to assess their role in the placement of young entry workers. Again, the issue is the comparison of substitute interventions with the informal network of relationships that operate for the majority.

Manpower services are not the only requirement for stability; small business now operates in a framework as complex, if not as extensive, as large enterprise. Accounting methods, inventory control, sources of supply, market potential, and numerous other technical issues loom as large for the small firm as for the large one. Some efforts have been made to offer needed advice on a volunteer basis, but the results of these efforts have not been disseminated. The feasibility of furnishing systematic management aids has not been established, but the notion has logical appeal as a way to enhance the stability of small units.

Job Redesign and New Careers

In the long run, major attention must be paid to the structuring of the increasing number of low-paid jobs in non-manufacturing. A situation may well arise in which beneath the thin stratum of well-paid professionals and managers, noncompeting groups will proliferate and the possibility of upward mobillty will be drastically decreased. One way to approach this problem is through job redesign, with improvement in articulation between adjacent levels. This type of intervention has been largely confined to the development of "New Careers in Human Services," but the possibility exists for much broader applications. The aim of the "New Careers" program is not only to open up jobs by reducing entry qualifications, but to provide prospects for continuing employment and advancement.

Practically speaking, the only arena in which "New Careers" has made headway is in government employment. New York City has made a commendable effort to experiment with several varieties of new hiring and training programs within the Civil Service. But even though government employment has increased and will continue to grow, very little has been done in the private sector in this respect, either in New York or elsewhere. New efforts are needed in several different directions. First of all, there is the possibility of providing promotional opportunities in situations now governed by rigid separation. Second, one might design intermediate jobs to build bridges over barriers that now prevent people from progressing. And third, it is possible to build purely nominal hierarchies in which rewards are given for length of satisfactory service so that upgrading does not altogether depend on assignment to more skilled duties.

Examples of these arrangements already exist. Thus, workers sometimes have the opportunity for optional moves within the firm, as in the rare instances of promotion from stock to sales positions in department stores. Again in department stores, District 65 of the Retail, Wholesale, and Department Store Workers Union has negotiated an upgrading scheme that in effect creates a wage progression for jobs designated as "heavy duty stock," even though they are not physically onerous in a literal sense. This scheme, in fact, only replicates similar arrangements in the utilities, manufacturing, and communications industries where a wide spread of wages offers the worker the opportunity to move up with respect to income even if his job duties remain unaltered.

The building of new levels of tasks has been largely directed to the services where a number of aides are now employed to relieve professionals of routine duties. The classic case, of course, is the practical nurse and the nurse's aide; unfortunately, however, it has proved difficult to build in ways for the aide to move up to the professional status or to approach its equivalent in pay, to say nothing of responsibility.

Despite all of the difficulties, it seems clear that in a security-minded society, ways will have to be found to regularize employment in the nongoods-producing sector that match traditional opportunities in goods production. The demand for the professionally trained has been maintained at a high level for so long that workers at the top can afford to behave more like classical entrepreneurs and to depend on the market for their rewards. But at the middle levels, and particularly in nonunionized clerical positions and at the low levels of the services, workers lack both job and income security. The problem becomes, then, one of providing opportunity within the framework of tasks that are being done, while allocating resources to new tasks as a way of expanding opportunity.

In New York City, the demographic trends are clear. The young are growing disproportionately among the population and of these young workers, increasing numbers are nonwhite or Puerto Rican. Some will take their place in the ranks of the professions, but by and large, no magic wand will rapidly or substantially alter the general trends. If young people are to become established, not only as workers but as citizens, the structure of opportunity must receive at least as much attention as the improvement of individuals.

7

The Peripheral Worker

ALTHOUGH a manpower strategy for the metropolis tends to concentrate upon the problem of matching the supply of workers who want full-time and stable jobs with the demand for such workers, an adequate strategy must take account of the fact that in the contemporary United States more than 4 out of every 10 individuals with work experience are not full-time, full-year workers.

This chapter is concerned with a group which we have termed "peripheral workers," who are located, as the term implies, on the fringes of the labor force and have widely differing contact with the world of work. Some have withdrawn from the labor force, others are chronically unemployed, while others have intermittent, part-time employment for part of the year, continuing part-time employment, or intermittent full-time employment.

Since the peripheral worker is not part of the regular full-time work force of employing institutions, less attention is paid to the problems which beset him. But just because his employment is irregular, because he is not protected to the same degree by the panoply of Social Security measures, because he does not have the same job security or seniority as the regular worker, his circumstances are often hard. In the past, there have been occasional instances when his lot provoked sufficient concern and indignation to bring about a radical change in the character of his work experience and his relationship to employing institutions. Casual and irregular employment, for example, characterized the waterfront until the recent past. As a result of the efforts of trade unions, longshoremen are now full-time workers.

Characteristics of the Peripheral Worker

Before we turn to the problems of the peripheral worker in the large city in general and in New York City in particular, we can gain some perspective by reviewing briefly the characteristics of this group in the nation as a whole. As Table 7 indicates, peripheral workers are, by and large, drawn from four distinct subgroups of the population. Women, youth, older workers, and nonwhites furnish a disproportionate number of peripheral workers.

As Table 8 demonstrates, the incidence of peripheral work experience is as variable if occupations are used as the basis of classification as when demographic categories are used. Since status in American life is so clearly a function of occupation, this is not at all surprising. As one rises on the occupational ladder, one's "stake" in a job increases. Indeed some of the occupations with the highest status provide the individual with an almost proprietary interest in his job. Movement in the other direction on the occupational ladder has in the past usually meant a weakening and eventual disappearance of any proprietary interest.

To sum up, peripheral workers are found primarily in four demographic groups: women, workers under twenty-four, workers over fifty-five, and nonwhites. They cluster in certain occupations, generally low skilled, low paid, and, above all, low status. They are much more commonly located in certain industries than in others, particularly in the service industries. They are rarely in evidence in industries where the typical firm is large, particularly where it has a highly bureaucratic structure. Finally the peripheral worker is very seldom found in such bureaucracies as federal administration.

Table 7. Work Experience of Selected Demographic Groups in the U.S., 1965

Demographic Group		Percent with Work Experience	Percentage Distribution of Those with Work Experience		
			Full-Time Jobs		Part-Time Jobs
Sex and Color	Age		50 to 52 weeks	1 to 26 weeks	
Male, white	25–44	98.3	82.3	2.7	2.2
Male, all	35–44	97.8	84.1	2.3	2.1
Female	35–44	45.4	45.8	11.3	29.0
Youth	18–19	74.8	14.7	35.0	39.6
	20–24	78.2	45.8	21.4	14.9
Older workers	60–64	62.2	63.5	6.0	16.3
	60–69	37.5	43.1	10.2	35.5
	70 and over	15.3	31.0	9.2	52.3
Male, nonwhite	25–44	94.6	71.3	5.6	5.6
Female, nonwhite	25–44	65.4	41.1	15.3	24.9

Source: Special Labor Force Report No. 76, *Work Experience of the Population in 1965*, U.S. Department of Labor, U.S. Government Printing Office, 1967, Table A-1, Table A-8.

Although we have emphasized that peripheral workers cluster in specific demographic groups, in specific indus-

Table 8. Percent Distribution of Individuals with Work Experience, U.S., by Occupation, 1965

	Male Distribution			Female Distribution		
	Full-Time Jobs		Part-Time Jobs	Full-Time Jobs		Part-Time Jobs
	50 to 52 weeks	1 to 26 weeks		50 to 52 weeks	1 to 26 weeks	
WHITE-COLLAR OCCUPATIONS						
Professional, technical, and kindred workers	77.6	5.4	6.2	41.8	13.5	21.9
Farmers and farm managers	77.3	2.1	15.1	38.3	3.4	52.3
Managers, officials, and proprietors (except farm)	88.5	2.2	3.6	64.9	7.8	16.5
Clerical and kindred workers	71.6	8.7	12.4	51.1	14.9	21.8
Sales workers	63.2	3.7	25.9	28.6	12.9	50.7

BLUE COLLAR OCCUPATIONS

Craftsmen, foremen, and kindred workers	74.1	5.3	5.1	53.0	9.1	18.9
Operatives and kindred workers	66.1	8.3	8.9	44.6	20.8	12.1
Durable goods	70.4	8.2	3.0	50.5	20.6	4.2
Nondurable goods	71.2	9.0	3.5	44.7	22.9	8.1
Other industries	56.2	9.8	20.4	37.6	16.0	31.1
Private household workers	—	—	—	15.0	8.9	70.9
Service workers (except private household)	56.1	9.8	23.1	29.9	19.3	34.6
Waiters, cooks, and bartenders	45.1	11.2	29.5	21.1	21.9	37.5
Farm laborers and foremen	24.7	20.0	45.8	8.7	18.4	66.4
Laborers (except farm and mine)	38.4	17.0	27.9	33.1	23.1	28.9

Source: *Work Experience of the Population in 1965*, Table A-5.

tries, and in specific occupations, it is important to note that in almost all demographic groups a considerable proportion of the workers are full-time, full-year employees. For example, we have noted that the nonwhite male worker is more apt to be a peripheral worker than the white male, but among the nonwhite male workers aged twenty-five to forty-four who had work experience during 1965, about 7 out of 10 were full-year, full-time employees.

This is so even though a much higher proportion of non-whites are located in the lower status occupations where one would expect a high proportion of peripheral work. In other words, there is evidence that nonwhite workers in general strive to achieve full-time and full-year status.

Peripheral Work in the Metropolis

Special cross-tabulations have been made, utilizing the 1-1000 tapes of the 1960 Census of Population to isolate the work experience of the population of the large metropolis in general and of the large metropolis in the Northeast in particular. The important story that the 1-1000 tapes have to tell concerns the relationship of the underlying pattern of peripheral work experience to the degree of urbanization and location of urban centers. The story is simple. In 1960 the nonwhite subgroups of the population, whether classified by age, sex, or marital status, were in a predominant number of cases less apt to be peripheral in the central cities of 1 million or more than in the other geographical subdivisions. The differences were not great between these largest centers of population and other urban centers, but they occur so often as to suggest that, at least until 1960, the largest urban centers provided more stable employment patterns for the nonwhite than the rest of the country. Unfortunately the available statistical data do not tell us whether *within* the central cores of the great cities of the country, particularly the central city of New York, the percentage of the labor force that has had primarily peripheral work experience has increased on the whole or for particular groups of the population. The large shifts in population that have occurred in the recent past, the major changes in the location of jobs, and a host of other factors in the situation make it hazardous to assume that the situation that obtained in 1960 in the large cities, particularly in their central cores, has not worsened for the peripheral worker and particularly for the nonwhite peripheral worker.

A considerable proportion of peripheral work is made up of personal services. As the middle and upper income groups move out of the central areas of the cities to suburbs, the location of this kind of peripheral work tends to move along with the consumers of personal services. The burgeoning world of consumer services that has sprung up in suburbia in the last few decades has shifted the location of innumerable peripheral work opportunities out of the central cities into the outlying suburbs.

A considerable proportion of those workers who have traditionally performed the more menial personal services has not moved to the suburbs. The day laborer is usually unable to afford housing in suburbia, and if he is nonwhite he is effectively blocked by segregated housing. The domestic servant, one of the most peripheral of workers, also finds an increasing distance (and even greater difficulty in traversing this distance) between where she lives and where the demand for her services is located. The phenomenon of "reverse commuting," a flow of labor from the central city to the suburb, is heavily weighted with nonwhites who have discovered employment opportunities in the suburbs but who have been unable to find adequate housing there. The wage rates that are paid to those who perform personal services in the suburbs are high, partly to reimburse those who must make costly and time-consuming journeys. Since personal services of this sort have traditionally earned low wages, the suburban dweller is frequently unwilling to pay what seems to him to be "exorbitant" rates for menial labor. Often he prefers to substitute capital for labor in the form of highly mechanized kitchens, large amounts of prepared foods, power lawnmowers, and do-it-yourself kits.

Within the central cities themselves, peripheral work experience in the past has been offered by specialized small manufacturing firms which have clustered in specific areas in order to reap the advantages of the external economies of location and a readily available labor supply that could be hired and fired with ease.

New York City has provided *par excellence* external economies for many industries, in particular the apparel trades clustering together in the very heart of the city, the garment center. Although the apparel industries have generally offered full-time employment, individual firms have customarily hired their production workers for relatively short periods of time. The pronounced seasonality of the industry as a whole, the "boom or bust" characteristics of individual firms in the high-style segments of the industry, make flexibility of output the first requirement of the firm. As a result the primary characteristic of employment for production workers in almost all branches of the apparel industry is intermittency.

Indeed, it has often been asserted that the system of un-

employment compensation operates to offer a partial subsidy to highly seasonal industries, such as the apparel industry, in areas where state unemployment compensation is
relatively liberal and the administration of the system efficient and rapid. At the same time, such industries become
heavy employers of individuals in demographic subgroups
more prone to peripheral work experience. Historically, the
apparel industries have employed immigrant labor. Today
the tendency is to increase employment of the new "immigrants," Negroes and Puerto Ricans, particularly women
from these subgroups.

Small-scale firms which locate in New York City to take
advantage of external economies offered by the wide range
of producer services available are not, of course, confined
to the apparel industries. Approximately one quarter of the
total employment in New York City is accounted for by
manufacturing industries, and, as late as 1956, considerably more than one half of these jobs were in industries
where the average employment of each firm did not exceed
60 workers. Less than 1 out of 10 workers in manufacturing
was employed in an industry where the average employment per firm exceeded 250. The relatively small size of
manufacturing firms in New York City is in part accounted
for by the fact that many manufacturing firms located in the
city are highly specialized, while many others perform subcontracting roles. Flexibility of output is a prime requirement for a considerable proportion of these small manufacturing firms.

The extremely large pool of skilled and semiskilled workers in the New York City area together with the highly developed system of private and public employment agencies
make it relatively easy for these small manufacturing firms

to vary their labor inputs. Such firms tend to maintain a cadre of highly skilled employees, adding and subtracting production workers as the flow of orders dictates. Although these semiskilled production workers in manufacturing may have fairly continuous work experience particularly when the national economy is functioning at a high level, it is rarely continuous work experience in one firm but rather a sequence of jobs with differing firms in related manufacturing industries.

Such a system does not develop strong commitments between employee and employer. Instead, the reverse attitude is desirable on both sides. The individual worker must be prepared for the abrupt termination of employment while the diverse employment opportunities offered by countless manufacturing firms make it desirable that he be willing to leave a firm if he learns of a better job. And the employer wants to be able to introduce a worker at a moment's notice into his production line and to terminate his employment by nightfall if he is unable to meet production quotas.

Historically the pool of semiskilled and unskilled workers who have made possible the high degree of flexibility characteristic of many New York manufacturing firms was to a large extent drawn from the flow of immigrants. The migration of large numbers of Puerto Ricans and southern Negroes to New York in the past few decades has partly filled the vacuum caused by the cessation of immigration from Europe. Small-scale manufacturing firms throughout the city now utilize a high proportion of Negroes and Puerto Ricans as production workers. The primary characteristic of the employment relationship in many of these firms is the lack of commitment of the worker to firm, occupation, or industry. Moreover, workers in many of these small-scale firms do not have trade-union affiliation (this is particularly true of the small-scale metal-fabricating plants in the area) and therefore lack the status and tenure which trade unions strive to attain for their members.

A final comment about the employment characteristics of the small-scale firm. If it is a manufacturing industry which requires a high degree of labor skill, there is a tendency to a rigid bifurcation of the personnel into two groups. One group, highly skilled and overwhelmingly white, is the cadre around which the plant is organized. The cadre is usually small and, since one of its functions is to integrate the semi-skilled or unskilled worker into production, it tends to be paternalistic and/or authoritarian towards the shifting group of production workers. This latter group is frequently Puerto Rican or nonwhite and often has low educational achievement. Instructions are therefore oral, relations with authority are direct and personal, friction is inevitable, and one result of this friction is the quick termination of employment on the initiative of either the employer or the employee.

Another area in which a large number of peripheral workers, both part time and intermittent, is found is the varied group of service occupations. It is in the services, also, that a wide variety of work schedules are found. Just as in retail sales, many services have to be offered to the consumer when the consumer wants them. This, of course, does not apply as much to producer services, where work schedules are in large part derived from the schedules of the industries they serve. However, some producer services are performed when the plant or office is not in operation. Many maintenance and cleaning operations, for example, must be performed at night.

A large proportion of these service occupations are not highly skilled, and many of them are among the most menial occupations in contemporary society. A number of them tend to cluster in the larger cities, especially in New York. Thousands of kitchen workers, countermen, janitors, elevator operators, charwomen and cleaners, waiters, ushers, and similar workers find more-or-less casual employment in large cities. New York has a high proportion of these workers because of its relatively large number of restaurants, apartment houses, and office buildings.

Very few of these service workers can look forward to an orderly career progression from low skill to high skill, from low wages to high wages, above all from casual employments experience to secure tenure. Many service occupations, because of such factors as irregular work schedules and late hours, have long attracted unattached individuals. The unattached male worker is far more apt to have a peripheral work experience than the male worker who has a family.

Among the industries and occupations that are characterized by a high degree of peripheral work experience, the construction industry occupies a peculiar position. Within the construction industry we must distinguish between the status of the highly skilled craftsmen and the large numbers of semiskilled and unskilled laborers who perform the myriad carrying, helping, and cleanup jobs. In recent years these menial tasks have been increasingly performed by nonwhites, and it seems probable that the intermittent character of construction work bears somewhat more heavily upon the laborer in the construction industry than upon craft workers.

A major employer of labor in New York City are the central offices of major corporations located in the city. The special characteristics of employment in these offices requires separate attention. In the first place, the central office employs two very different types of labor. On the one hand, it employs a large number of executives and specialists whose work histories tend to form an orderly progression of increasing commitment to individual firms and in many cases to specific occupations within firms. On the other hand, this group of strategic employees is surrounded by a much larger group of clerical assistants, primarily female, whose work histories are apt to have a very different profile. Some of these women clerical workers, it is true, develop strong attachments to particular firms and have lengthy tenure. These tend to be either unmarried or childless women. A much larger proportion of the women employed in central offices are young high-school graduates who work full time until they marry and start their families.

Until very recently, the managers of large central offices in New York have been reluctant to use part-time, middle-aged women employees, even though they have complained that they are unable to secure an adequate supply of well-trained and reliable younger full-time clerical help. A study made by Jane Schwartz for the Alumnae Advisory Center, *Part-Time Employment,* documents the unwillingness of some employers to hire educated part-time women employees. The argument generally put forth by personnel managers is that a central office, as a large bureaucratic structure, must have common rules governing such matters as work schedules. The part-time worker, necessarily an exception, does not fit into an efficient office operation which must process in an orderly, sequential, and controlled fashion a large and varied amount of information, instruction, and orders.

Although executives frequently display marked antipathy to part-time employees, the use of part-time office workers, according to Mrs. Schwartz, is in fact a common practice. Indeed, many specialized firms have sprung up which supply part-time secretarial and clerical help on a contract basis. The use of part-time office workers on a continuing basis is partly a result of the very real difficulties experienced by large offices in their attempts to secure a sufficient number of mature, well-trained women to provide a disciplined core of clerical support for executives. It may well be that central offices located in the inner city have found that a considerable proportion of their usual clerical labor supply, the white female high-school graduate, has moved to the suburbs. A reluctance to use nonwhites in place of whites on a large scale has resulted in an effort to utilize part-time middle-aged white women with clerical experience in place of the customary young full-time white girls.

Some Policy Implications

What are some of the fundamental policy implications which emerge from an overall consideration of peripheral work experience in the metropolis? Several seem to stand out. First of all, since peripheral work experience covers immensely broad and varied fields of human activity, it is essential that a general manpower policy for the metropolis consider as thoroughly as possible the spillover effects of any measure. Specifically, a measure intended to stabilize work experience in general might have the unintended effect of drying up sources of peripheral work experience which are essential for many individuals. Part-time or intermittent employment is a desirable option for teenagers, for college students, for post-graduate students, for married women, for mothers with young children, for older workers, or for individuals whose life style does not include total commitment to work. A healthy economy should provide sufficient peripheral work experience opportunities to match the demand for such work.

Indeed, an attentive government will examine policies which do not have a direct manpower purpose to determine their impact on peripheral workers. Urban renewal, for example, may inadvertently eliminate certain types of peripheral work which have traditionally provided income and constructive activity for some young people.

Peripheral work has often been an important concomitant of progress through high school and college for young middle-class whites, providing them with important training in the development of mature attitudes towards work, varied opportunities for exploration of attractive career possibilities, and necessary financial support for heavy and prolonged educational investment. For the nonwhite, however, early peripheral work experience has too often meant that lifetime work will be predominantly peripheral in character, a succession of casual employment experience, low paid, and more important, with low skills and little on-the-job training components.

In any case, it is likely that great urban centers will find it increasingly difficult to furnish, within their own geographical boundaries, the kind of peripheral work, particularly summer employment, which in the past has been part of the crucial process whereby young persons explore the world of work and at the same time help to finance their education. At the other end of the age scale, the great metropolis may be unable to furnish adequate amounts of peripheral work experience for older workers who desire part-time or part-year employment to supplement their retirement income or to ease the shock of an otherwise too abrupt retirement. The presence of large numbers of elderly individuals in the great cities, particularly women who have no family ties and inadequate incomes, suggests that an increase in the opportunities for peripheral work for this group would be desirable.

Public policy, therefore, should be directed to maintaining and even enlarging the opportunities for peripheral work where this plays a constructive role in the life of an individual. In particular, it is important that adequate opportunities for constructive peripheral work be provided for the teenager brought up in slum areas. Since such a young person does not ordinarily have much access to work within the boundaries of the urban slum, serious thought should be given to methods of providing such work for him, particularly during summer months.

In smaller communities and in the suburbs, access to summer employment is apt to be through informal and personal relationships. There does not seem to be any obvious substitute for such supportive relationships to help introduce the slum child to work. Perhaps schools can do more to develop programs and guidance in this area. It is possible, however, that summer and part-time work programs for the urban teenager should be kept quite separate from the school system since the slum child, particularly the school drop-out, is apt to associate a work program carried out under the aegis of the schools with lack of success in schoolwork and with a sense that school-related work experiences inevitably represent an artificial rather than a real experience with work. It is essential that programs which offer work experience to teenagers from slum areas should be so structured as to lead to eventual full-time commitment to work. The worst possible result is when the early employment experience of the slum teenager confirms that he is destined to repeat the casual and irregular employment experience of many adults in his environment.

We have emphasized the importance of sufficient constructive peripheral work for specific groups, teenagers, older workers, and women who want to supplement their family income. But there is another, less attractive, side to peripheral work. Peripheral workers in New York are concentrated heavily in occupations which require little skill, and they are often employed by small firms that offer little training to part-time or intermittent employees. Large, heavily capitalized firms generally employ full-time, full-year workers. These large firms are apt to be strongly unionized and to use formal hiring and firing procedures. It is hard for workers with little education, little training, and a history of irregular and casual employment to surmount the barriers raised by these procedures.

Several important consequences follow from this general situation. A worker who is twenty-five years old and whose employment experience has been largely peripheral may be on a dead-end road with regard to a work career. He is less apt than a full-time, full-year worker to have received any training, more apt to be a victim of seasonal ebbs and flows of production, more apt to find himself superfluous in a recession, and more apt to be employed by small firms subject to wide variations in output and short lifetimes. He is less protected by public policy designed to maintain income or to shield him from the consequences of illness, accident, or old age. He is less able to count upon a strong union to protect him from arbitrary and abrupt termination of employment. He is more dependent upon casual sources for information about job opportunities.

Finally he is more apt to withdraw from the labor force entirely if his work experience becomes increasingly peripheral. Although no definitive statistics are available upon which to base generalizations about the process by which a worker becomes increasingly less committed to work while he is still in the prime age group (twenty-five to fifty-four), it is clear that workers who have been full-time, full-year workers do not give up their commitment to work easily. It seems likely, however, that many of the recent migrants from the South to the great urban centers of the North, already highly peripheral in their work experience because of their having been pushed off the land by technological change, drop out of the labor market entirely if their work experience in the city falls below a minimum level. In the South, particularly in the smaller communities, they were part of a labor pool which depends upon an informal network of information for occasional work. In the large Northern cities, these recent migrants have little access to this kind of information and no experience in using more formal types of information about job opportunities.

What, then, can public and private policy do for these individuals, all too frequently nonwhite, all too frequently the most defenseless members of society because of age or family problems or their primarily peripheral work experience? Can anything be done to break the chain of circumstances which fastens casual and irregular employment upon those individuals whose lives in many other respects are also subject to great hazards?

Since peripheral work status is apt to be associated with low levels of skills, low educational attainment, and the absence of any significant formal or on-the-job training, since it is associated frequently with low wage rates and even lower yearly income, manpower policies designed to improve the situation of the peripheral worker must be both broad in range and deep in effect. Like most specific manpower policies, success depends in the last analysis upon a high level of employment in the nation as a whole. Indeed the problem of the peripheral worker does not really exist as a specific problem until low rates of unemployment in general are attained. It is only in a tight labor market that it is possible to distinguish clearly the groups in the population which do not have access to sufficient voluntary peripheral work from those groups which seem to be enmeshed in peripheral work experience unwillingly and at the cost of a fuller commitment to more productive work.

Assuming that the economy as a whole is able to maintain high rates of employment, can we expect that the problems of the peripheral worker will disappear in large urban centers? In these circumstances, the problem of the peripheral worker in the city becomes a specific aspect of the general problem of structural unemployment, a facet of the larger problem of insuring that the supply of workers of all types, including those who desire partial rather than full employment, matches the demand for such workers.

The available evidence seems to indicate that high levels of employment in the country as a whole are not likely to eliminate the particular problems of the peripheral workers in New York City. It may be possible for some nonwhite peripheral workers to relocate in the suburbs where more stable employment opportunities exist, but it is hardly likely that the flow of nonwhites out of the central cities can be sufficiently rapid to bring down quickly the very high rates of peripheral employment in the ghetto areas.

If present rates of unemployment, underemployment, and nonparticipation in the labor force of the nonwhite worker in the great city ghettoes continue, they threaten to increase to truly dangerous degrees the sense of despair and the sense of alienation and demoralization among this group. Rather than place all our trust in the long-run beneficent effects of high national employment rates on the situation of the nonwhite urban worker, wisdom and justice dictate that we begin to plan and carry out programs to create more stable employment opportunties for the nonwhite urban worker *where he presently lives.* Public and private manpower policy might properly be directed towards locating public and private enterprises with stable employment practices in areas where the peripheral worker now lives. It might prove sensible to put as much effort and financial support into the provision of stable employment opportunities in slum areas as into public housing in these areas. It is of particular importance that workers who are trapped in a sequence of peripheral work experiences finally be offered employment which contains a considerable component of on-the-job training to make up for their relative deprivation in this respect.

There are indeed indications that powerful political and nonpolitical forces are beginning to feel that the solution to the employment problems of the great cities of America must include intensive efforts to establish public and private enterprises within the boundaries of slum areas. It seems certain that such efforts will succeed only if imaginative techniques of subsidy are developed. At present, powerful economic forces make the location of industrial and commercial activity in the central cities less and less attractive to private enterprise.

On the other hand, if the low productivity of many individuals in slum areas is due to a combination of inadequate education (it is almost a certainty that the Negro in a large city who is a recent migrant from rural Southern areas is educationally deprived) and inadequate opportunities for job training because of casual and irregular employment experience, there is a powerful economic argument that supports temporary protection or subsidy of their employment in industries and occupations which, by offering a large component of training, will increase their productivity. But, as with "infant industry" tariffs, the problem of subsidized employment designed to lead to an increase in the productivity of workers centers around the appropriate moment for the eventual removal of the subsidy. A successful subsidy program will lead to increases in productivity. The gains from such increases accrue either to the employer or to the employees themselves. The subsidy properly should decrease as labor productivity increases, until finally the productivity of the workers has reached a point where it is economically profitable to employ them in industries which provide stable employment at satisfactory unsubsidized wages.

However, once a subsidized employment program designed to make it possible for peripheral workers to become full-time, full-year employees of profitable large-scale firms has been set in motion, it will not be easy to persuade either employers or employees to accept a reduction in subsidies.

If the subsidy is relatively invisible, it will be even more difficult to remove it when it is no longer justified. At the same time, there are real pressures upon political and business leaders to make subsidies take just such invisible forms—tax abatement, writing down of land values, and so forth—because of the public's deep-seated objections to direct wage subsidies, which always seem inequitable to unsubsidized workers.

Programs to lead the peripheral worker from irregular and low-paid work to more stable and more productive employment should not be limited, however, to the direct creation of jobs for such workers through various types of subsidy programs. There are a number of other possible routes which can ease the transition of the peripheral worker to full-time, full-year status.

One of the most promising possibilities is the provision of fuller information to peripheral workers about stable employment opportunities. Because an individual is peripheral and therefore has little direct personal contact with workers whose employment status is full-time and full-year, because his educational background does not permit him to apply through employment agencies, which assume some degree of literacy, ordinary channels of information about job opportunities may be closed to him. Just as the Census Bureau has found that it must develop new techniques of survey, much more searching, much more personal, and therefore much more expensive and more sophisticated, in order to establish minimally adequate contact with the nonwhite male in slum areas, so employment agencies, public and private, must be induced to make much more direct and personal approaches to such workers. The public employment agencies have not traditionally been fully satisfactory vehicles for providing employment opportunities. Meanwhile private employment agencies have taken their cues very much from the employers to whom they refer job applicants.

If private employment agencies could look forward to some means of recouping the additional costs of providing information to peripheral workers about stable employment opportunities, their efforts to recruit such workers for full-time, full-year job opportunities could be expected to increase. Economists have recently recognized that there are frequently quite heavy "search" costs involved in matching a job with a worker. In the past these costs have largely been borne either by the employer or the employee, or shared between them. "Search" costs for the peripheral worker trying to find full-time, full-year work are relatively heavy, and the employer is usually not willing to pay an appreciable proportion of these costs to find such a worker.

Public and private manpower policy must take into account the fact that many of the recent immigrants from the rural South, after being displaced from the land, formed for a time part of a floating pool of casual labor which collected in the smaller towns and villages of the South. An active search for regular work in these communities was often fruitless. The employer simply went to wherever a pool of casual workers was to be found and chose as many workers as he needed. Such workers, transplanted to the Northern cities, have little or no experience with the process of formal application for work, and they frequently lack the elementary documents and work history that personnel officers of large firms use as screening devices. For these workers, to seek work actively means to assemble each morning at the informal "shape up" point. Since there is no real

equivalent of this kind of a labor market in the Northern
city, these individuals tend to drop out of the labor force
entirely. Their work experience in the North may be limited
to an occasional job of shoveling snow when the Sanitation
Department must suddenly recruit a large number of temporary workers.

Certainly one of the most important means of improving the employment status of the peripheral worker lies
in a change in the practices of many personnel offices.
Chapter 5 in this volume documents the inappropriate-
ness of educational achievement as a screening device
for many types of work. However, as long as personnel
officers use a high-school diploma as a screening device,
many peripheral workers are condemned to casual employment by small-scale firms where a diploma is not required.
The barrier to employment represented by the lack of a
high-school diploma is a particularly heavy burden for the
nonwhite peripheral worker. If he is a recent immigrant
from the rural South, the likelihood that he has a high-
school diploma is small indeed.

But it is not enough that personnel officers use realistic
educational requirements. Another screening device frequently used today is the work history of the applicant. In
many cases the peripheral worker has, essentially, no work
history from the point of view of many personnel officers. It
is impossible for the applicant to reconstruct his employment record. His work experience is so diverse, so full of
gaps, that the ordinary employment application form is ir-
relevant. In addition to being unable to fill out satisfactorily
the employment application, the peripheral worker frequently finds that he does not have many of the attributes of
middle-class American life which increasingly are taken for

granted by personnel offices and employment agencies. He does not have a driver's license, he has no bank account. Moreover, if his work history is investigated, it is apt to include positive reasons for his rejection, such as a record of garnishment of wages or arrest.

Since the practices of personnel offices are generally designed to reduce the risk that any worker who is hired will be unsatisfactory, it might be possible to develop more flexible personnel policies if some of the costs of unsatisfactory employment decisions were borne, not by the firm, but by the public at large. Essentially part of the costs of personnel offices should be considered by the firm to be the equivalent of an insurance premium. Where the risk of failure of proper performance by a new employee is substantial, the practice of bonding workers has already developed. Perhaps an analogous procedure could be extended to cover the applicant who seems to be too much of a risk for the average large-scale employer of blue-collar and lower-level white-collar workers.

Certainly it should be possible for public policy to devise ways by which the most obvious of barriers to employment, such as lack of a driver's license, could be surmounted. But where the obstacle to employment is a record of arrest or of garnishment of wages, both of which might indicate to the ordinary personnel officer a higher risk, public agencies might properly be asked to cover the risk.

The foregoing suggestions represent only a few of the possible ways of reducing the incidence of peripheral work where it is clearly an undesirable aspect of a person's work life. We do not claim that any of these suggestions are necessarily feasible, politically or otherwise. At the same time, it is almost certain that imagination and sympathy, coupled with a sense of the urgency of the problem and the need for bold innovation, can devise effective means of regularizing the employment experience of thousands of workers who at present seem condemned to a casual and unsatisfactory relationship to the world of work. The revolution that has taken place within a few decades in the status of the long-shoreman shows what can be achieved. But that same record indicates that a transformation in the status of the peripheral worker will not be cheap, and that it requires very careful planning, vigorous execution, and watchful concern for its long-term effects upon the total economy of the area.

Conclusion

Basically, public and private manpower policy for the peripheral worker should be flexible and specific at one and the same time. It should be based upon a clear understanding of the specific demographic groups that are most subject to peripheral work experience. It should recognize that specific areas of the city suffer more severely than does the city as a whole from the disadvantageous effects of undesirable peripheral work experience which are associated with high rates of unemployment in general and with unstable life patterns. Recognizing who is affected and where they are located provides the base for an attack on the problem.

At the same time, it is important that public and private policy understand that peripheral work experience is highly desirable, indeed essential, for certain groups, particularly the young and the old and women who need to supplement their income with part-time employment.

The problem of the peripheral worker in the nation as a

whole and in the large city in particular is essentially one of matching the supply of workers with the demand and in such a way that inequitable burdens are not placed on specific individuals or groups. Traditionally, the peripheral worker in American society has been drawn largely from immigrant groups. In the past, many of these immigrants settled in the great cities of the nation where usually their children, and often they themselves, were able to make the transition from peripheral work status to the well-paid stable employment which characterizes such a high proportion of white adult male American workers today. Some cities, particularly New York, made very strong efforts to assist these early immigrants to make the transition from a low status in the world of work to a higher rank.

The stream of immigration into the large cities of the country today is no longer from foreign lands. It has in the recent past consisted of a vast flow of Southern Negroes and Puerto Ricans into the same cities which earlier absorbed the immigrant from Europe and from Asia. The challenge to the American city today is to enable the adults who have made up this stream to become full-time, full-year workers and to provide opportunities for their children to enter the same kind of occupations and industries which have made possible the enormous improvement in status and income that the white American worker has achieved in the past few decades.

On the one hand, the task is made immensely difficult by the intransigent patterns of discrimination that surround the nonwhite worker, by the unconscionable delay in granting him elementary rights of access to education, residence, and employment, and by the resulting accumulation of bitterness and the breakdown of communication. On the other hand, it is probable that this is the last time that the American city will be asked to absorb immigrants on anything like this scale. The effort, however costly it may be, needs to be made in all probability only this once. The immigrants to the great cities of America are already American citizens, most of them already know the language, and they have an immense reservoir of potential skills and energy which they themselves, and the country along with them, need desperately to tap.

8

The Hard-to-Employ:
European Experience

THE term "hard-to-employ" is an awkward but useful label to designate those who are neither employable nor unemployable. This term also is a reaction against the unjust and harsh tendency during the Great Depression to discard many jobless workers on a rubbish heap of "unemployables." As recently as the 1950s, West Germany analyzed its unemployment in this way, only to find substantial numbers of the so-called unemployables moving into jobs as the demand for labor soared, and such classifications were abandoned. In short, the concept of the "hard-to-employ" is a recognition of the relativity of all judgments about employability and marginality. It is also more optimistic and policy-oriented than a sharp division into the employables and the unemployables.

To be designated as "hard-to-employ," it is not necessary to be unemployed, although it is the unemployed or underemployed segment which is likely to command the greatest public attention. Workers with good and long work histories can become hard-to-employ through aging or a deterioration of their skills and health; while they are working, they may be called the "hard-to-reemploy." Another subgroup is the "hard-to-place"; they perform satisfactorily once the resistance of the employer is overcome. These include cases where prejudice in hiring is based on race, appearance, or any attribute which does not affect actual or potential work performance. The core of the hard-to-employ are those with multiple physical, mental, or social disabilities which make them difficult to place and to employ.

The number of hard-to-employ unemployed varies from place to place and over time, depending on the state of the demand for labor, employers' attitudes, and manpower and related programs. But other factors also influence the size of the category. If a country (or a city) has a heterogeneous population, which is characterized by great disparities in the quality of education, health services, and housing, and a marked inequality in the distribution of income, it is probable that the incidence of the hard-to-employ will be greater than in a country such as Denmark or Sweden, where the population is homogeneous and the income distribution less variable.

It must be borne in mind that the classification "hard-to-employ" is influenced by local circumstances. For example, in Great Britain where regional unemployment problems have persisted throughout the postwar period of low overall unemployment, Employment Service officers in areas of relatively high unemployment tend to adopt the local employers' stiffer standards of acceptability. They designate workers in Wales and Scotland as "hard-to-employ" who would not be given that designation in London or the Midlands areas of labor shortage.

Some illustrations of the hard-to-employ in Western Europe in the active files in 1965–66 indicate every variety which might be found in New York City. The cases do not divide neatly into groups, but the reader will observe a certain typology in the listing.

A West Indian of twenty-eight, unemployed for eleven months in Britain, received unemployment benefits (for himself and family) which were very close to his unskilled wages and left him unwilling to look for such work. He had attended an evening training course for a skilled job, but dropped out because he thought his color was a bar to employment.

A Polish man in England, with a fairly good command of spoken English and a good commercial education in Poland, lacked the standard of commercial education prevailing in England and could obtain only manual work, which was distasteful to him.

In the Netherlands, a man of forty-one was rejected for several jobs because he was a known homosexual.

A German attorney, disbarred for using his client's money, could not obtain any work with what he felt to be appropriate social or economic status. He began to drink and have marital troubles, making him hard-to-employ in other work as well.

A Dutchman of forty-two with eleven children could work only irregularly as a port inspector for small firms because the insurance-conscious doctors of the large firms which could provide permanent employment turned him down on physical grounds, although his disability was not serious.

A twenty-year-old German had dropped out of school in sixth grade, forfeiting his opportunity to obtain vocational training. At fourteen he was an errand boy and at eighteen became a truck driver with a third-class license. By twenty he had changed jobs seventeen times, seeking high seasonal and overtime pay to cover the costs of a too expensive car.

A London boy of eighteen, the product of a broken home, held an unskilled job for two years after completing primary school. He then turned beatnik, lived in a lodging house for down-and-outers, wore his hair to his shoulders, and looked so dirty that he could not be sent for job interviews.

A British capstan operator of forty-eight was discharged as redundant after twenty-nine years with a single employer. He worked only two weeks in the next eighteen months, and began to lose confidence in his ability to maintain the required speed on production work, since he had previously been on slower-paced experimental work.

A London self-employed picture-frame maker, aged fifty-nine, saw little prospect of employment after giving up his dying business.

A redundant British foreman of fifty-seven was reluctant to accept work at lower pay and status.

Speaking so little English that a friend had to interpret for him at the London Employment Service, a Polish man of fifty-four proved to be almost illiterate in Polish as well. He came from a peasant background, had little ambition, and wanted to work only intermittently. He was eligible only for simple manual jobs where Polish was spoken by his superior.

In Stockholm, a man, forty-two, had worked irregularly at heavy construction jobs. Born with a speech and hearing defect, he had attended a school for mentally retarded children but had not learned to read or write. This handicap made him lose several jobs and to appear bad-tempered and lacking in self-control at interviews and at work.

A mental defective of thirty-five, who had not worked for nine years, appeared for an interview.

A skilled machinist, aged fifty-three, had to give up factory work because of bad health.

An unmarried British man of thirty-four, who had not worked for six years, came to an interview and delivered a long monologue on red and blue pigeons. Subsequently he made impromptu appearances at the interview office, giving unintelligible discourses. To suggestions that he see a doctor, he declared that he was quite fit and had no need for medical or psychiatric attention.

A Dutchman of fifty-six, who had once been committed to an institution because of chronic alcoholism, appeared to be highly disturbed at his interview. He suddenly announced in a matter-of-fact way that he intended to murder his wife and daughter and then commit suicide.

A British truck driver of forty-two, who had served one employer for eighteen years, lost all interest in work when his wife entered a mental hospital.

A Swedish woman, whose husband became an alcoholic, began to work irregularly after a long period of steady employment. She looked unkempt and broke down in tears in front of prospective employers.

A man whose wife had deserted him and several small children stayed at home to care for them, living on relief.

A well-dressed man living in a fairly expensive manner did not wish to discuss his finances and rejected all work suggestions. He was assumed to be drawing income from unreported jobs and/or illegal activities.

In the Midlands, a family consisting of two brothers and the son of one, all with prison records, did not report for the jobs provided by the Employment Service.

A retired member of the regular British Army continued to receive unemployment benefits because his total income from his army pension was unsatisfactory.

A German, thirty-four, was constantly on the run from court orders which attached his wages or had to give up work to serve prison sentences. He drank, had debts, and had been divorced *pro forma* from his wife who, with their four children, was on relief. He maintained a shabby room, but actually lived with his family.

In Britain, an unskilled manual worker of thirty-five had been unemployed for a year and a half. He had a prison record, held jobs only for a few weeks to a few months, and usually was discharged for poor performance, lateness, or absenteeism.

The repeated evidence that the hard-to-employ have complicating personal and social handicaps is not peculiar to Western Europe. Comparable data for New York City are available through the participation of the United States in a 1965 Organization of European Cooperation and Development (OECD) inquiry. Of the 174 New York City cases, only 29 were judged by the interviewers to be unemployed entirely because of economic circumstances. While the unemployed tended to blame their lack of work on the absence of jobs, the interviewers found a combination of other factors to be largely responsible—emotional disturbance and family troubles; inadequate training, skills, or performance; poor references; lack of literacy or comprehension of English; poor health; and indifference or unwillingness to work.

It is likely that the number and intensity of complicating factors increase as unemployment is prolonged in individual cases, and, as the unemployed group grows large, it is concentrated in a ghetto and assumes the form of a subculture. The hard-to-employ group in Western Europe is conspicuously free of disproportionate numbers of young people or those whose color or race might cause prejudice in hiring. The lack of skill or education also is relatively unimportant as a bar to employment if other disqualifying attributes are absent. Moreover, illiteracy is far less common in Western Europe than in the United States.

To Americans one of the most interesting questions is a negative one: why do not the West Europeans have our youth and minority unemployment problems? It would take us too far afield to attempt an answer here, but it can be said that deliberate manpower policies appear to be less important in the explanation than other factors such as demographic trends, labor supply-and-demand relationships, and certain institutional patterns and arrangements.

The hard-to-employ among the unemployed are most significant, both statistically and for manpower policy, when overall unemployment is low. As unemployment declines, the most employable workers are hired first and the hard-to-employ tend to form an increasing proportion of the residual unemployed. In addition, a tight labor market brings forth certain hard-to-employ workers who in other times do not even seek work.

Manpower officials acquire a new interest in the hard-to-employ when labor shortages appear. The hard-to-employ are part of the labor reserve which must be drawn into active employment to meet employers' demands, increase the national product, and restrain inflationary pressures on wages. The moral and financial welfare of the unemployed thus is linked with the national goal of full employment and the demand for labor in the economy. This is the stage which manpower policy in most Western European countries has reached.

In dealing with their hard-to-employ, the Western European countries have labor market advantages which New York City does not enjoy and which are not due to manpower policy as such. There is no doubt that postwar unemployment rates have been far lower in the nations of northwestern Europe than in the United States or in New York City. In fact, the United States considers itself at full employment at the same unemployment rate which arouses political indignation and demands for employment-creating measures in the Western European countries. Most of these nations have had unemployment rates of under 3 percent for a decade or more, and some rates have hovered around 1 or 2 percent for some years. Full or overfull employment has had the most salutary effect on unemployed who are designated as hard-to-employ. Many have been absorbed who would have remained a placement problem under looser labor market conditions. More important, a pool of disaffected unemployed has not developed.

The strong demand for labor in Europe relative to labor supply (which has grown at a slower rate in most countries than in the United States) has tended to minimize the jobless hard-to-employ population in the Western European countries. But the types of job vacancies also play an important part. In Europe, unskilled workers have been sought in great numbers, educational requirements have been low, and the largest number of vacancies has consistently been in manufacturing and construction work. These conditions, reminiscent of the United States of an earlier era, are not in conflict with observed tendencies in Western

Europe for employment to become automated and skilled and for service activities to grow at a faster pace than manufacturing. But in terms of sheer numbers of jobs, openings that would be suitable for the hard-to-employ have been relatively more available in Europe than in the United States in recent years.

Some indication of the job vacancy picture can be gleaned from recent statements about individual countries. A West German authority wrote of his nation: "In the case of heavy manual work, e.g., in the building industry, in agriculture, and in transportation, there are always vacancies, whereas in the case of commercial and clerical employment there is nearly always a surplus of labour available."

On the Netherlands, a team of OECD examiners observed: "The relative rates of vacancies for male workers are highest among the manual workers. . . . Large demands for manpower are reported for jobs where the educational requirements are low."

An American Labor Department official reported with surprise that Sweden had a high demand for blue-collar workers; Sweden is often said to come closest to the United States in employment patterns, technology, and business methods. In Britain, the Employment Service declared that illiteracy itself is not "a great handicap in obtaining unskilled work," nor is a prison record.

In France, a survey of vacancies was made in 1963 in order to place the Algerian repatriates. It showed that 51 percent of the job openings were for agricultural laborers and miners, 34 percent were in industry, and only 15 percent were in service occupations.

In fact, the numbers of employable hard-to-employ in Western Europe have not been sufficient to fill all the va-

cancies, and various arrangements to bring in foreign labor
have been made. No social concern has been evident over
either the low wage levels or the unrewarding type of work
available to most of the hard-to-employ or foreigners. Family allowances greatly assist low-paid workers who have
many children. However, programs to upgrade and place
individual workers at jobs which would utilize their highest
ability are an increasingly important part of the most advanced manpower policy in Western Europe. In this program, special attention is given to the hard-to-employ, but
the lure of ready jobs deters many from taking advantage of
these training opportunities.

An American might be tempted to say that the West
Europeans will have our scale of problems with the hard-to-
employ when their technological changes and labor-saving
methods approach the level now prevailing in the United
States. To this, the Europeans might reply that even with
their present easier situation they have adopted general social and economic policies and specific manpower programs
to minimize the difficulties of the hard-to-employ and that
they will adjust to future developments and anticipate and
alleviate the human and social problems attendant on economic progress. They feel that their experience and programs are relevant to American issues.

Some of the preventive and remedial manpower programs which have operated for some years in Western European countries have direct interest for New York City. In
particular we should study the anticipatory economic, social, and labor market measures which tend to forestall the
creation of a large group of hard-to-employ workers. Two
situations which have caused Western European countries
to act are highly relevant to New York City: the movement

of displaced or underemployed rural populations to urban and industrial life, and the immigration of nationals who have an unrestricted right of entry, such as characterizes Puerto Ricans with regard to the United States.

European manpower experts find it difficult to conceal their wonder that the United States has permitted such a massive exodus from Southern agriculture without establishing a series of programs of matching scale to cope with the displacement of millions of people. The fact that the migration to New York and other large cities in the North and West was caused not by the pull of new employment opportunities, but by the push off the land and rural stagnation makes the establishment of manpower and other programs even more urgent in European eyes.

The further fact that the unrestricted and undirected flooding of the large cities was in excess of job opportunities and available housing, both quantitatively and qualitatively, and the aggravation of these conditions by the high birth rates among the migrants, confirm the European belief that this is a major national problem requiring national initiative. To them, it seems that only limited success would follow local action alone, undertaken either by the impoverished areas of out-migration or the overburdened reception centers. New York City, they would say, should not be expected to cope with this major economic dislocation entirely alone. Nor should one city have to provide jobs and homes for 70 percent of the migrants from Puerto Rico.

Since the end of the outpouring from agricultural areas is not yet in sight, New York City has a current interest in preventive action, such as some Western European countries have taken. Several of these nations have had an even greater relative exodus from agriculture, mining, and forestry than the United States has experienced since the end of World War II. But they have had the advantage of fewer differences between their rural and urban populations with regard to levels of health, housing, education, vocational training and skills, and social and cultural habits. Nor has the adjustment of surplus rural populations in Europe been complicated by racial issues. While these circumstances have somewhat smoothed the European process of successful transfer out of agriculture, they have not eliminated the problems. Even the relative ease with which surplus rural workers have been placed in unskilled construction and manufacturing jobs has not made the Europeans complacent or ready to rely on the automatic adjustments of the market.

Without describing the program of any particular country, we can delineate the main types of action which have been followed in Europe and which might prove useful in the United States. Six complementary approaches can be distinguished: preparing rural people for change, directing and assisting mobility toward industrial and urban employment, regional development to provide alternative local employment, deliberate creation of public service jobs in areas of surplus labor, restrictions on further expansion of certain metropolitan centers, and improvement of the status and earnings of the remaining agricultural labor force.

The specific policies which affect the individual are in the first instance advance preparation and selection for transfer out of agriculture. Here a country buys out uneconomical small farms or makes resettlement loans or grants or gives special or supplementary pensions to older farmers. Basic remedial education, vocational guidance, and subsidized vocational training are offered *before* migration and within daily traveling distance of the farm community. Efforts are made to improve rural basic and vocational education for youngsters who will eventually leave agriculture. Full information is given on working and living conditions in other areas; socio-psychological guidance is offered. Provision is made for families who stay on the farm. Guidance and vocational training are offered during the military service period, a time when rural youths often decide not to return to farming.

The measures which direct the flow of migrants to places which have jobs and housing depend on a strong and well-informed employment service with extensive inter-area clearance and advance placement procedures. Financial assistance can be obtained to ease mobility. Housing is provided, subsidized, or built directly in areas of labor demand, and migrants are assisted to relocate. With regard to the concentration of migrants, a European observation is of interest in the American context. "Intermediate solutions between a ghetto existence and dispersion must be found, since segregation in a ghetto causes them to live in a closed circuit, whereas dispersion and consequent isolation accentuate the feeling of being uprooted."

One solution is the deliberate creation of new towns to relieve the pressures on the older centers and to provide suitable job opportunities for the migrants. These may be independent of or connected with area development programs which make it possible for displaced rural workers to continue to live in familiar surroundings.

Many Europeans believe that "by giving movement of industry priority over movement of manpower, arbitrary displacement and the human dramas resulting from it can be avoided." In France, Germany, the Netherlands, and

Belgium, programs to bring jobs to the workers have made it unnecessary for many to migrate. Many European workers prefer to spend several hours in daily commuting rather than move their place of residence, and a lack of housing in the job vicinity may reinforce the preference. To assist workers in this situation, governments and firms have developed high-speed, low-cost mass transportation schemes. Flemish workers who hold jobs in the Walloon areas of Belgium (and vice versa), French industrial workers who live in scattered farming areas in the Savoy mountains, and frontier workers who daily cross a national border to get to work, are among those for whom special transportation arrangements are made.

Since the very extensive area development programs to encourage private investment in centers of surplus labor have not provided a sufficient number of jobs for the unemployed, several Western European countries have supplemented these efforts with the direct creation of public service jobs for the older less mobile and less employable workers. Some of the jobs are designed to make the development areas more attractive to private capital. Again, the attempt is to prevent uprooting, with its social and human costs. In a variation of this, Sweden has sent some of its unemployed men from the north to work on public service projects in the busy south, hoping in this way to arrange a transfer to permanent employment.

One feature of European programs which is foreign to American policy is the limitation on the further growth of the major cities. The concept of planned and balanced growth suggests that the under-utilized resources of certain areas can be made productive without the inflationary pres-

sure that additions to capacity in the already strained
major production centers would create.

Analyses of the social costs and benefits of large metropolises lead to notions of optimum size and overexpansion of
cities. Thus, European countries have limited the growth of
their major cities by restrictions on additions or new facilities for certain kinds of economic activities. Limitations
on new housing construction as well as strict enforcement of
occupancy laws prevent the cities from filling up with those
who cannot be fitted into their economic life. The restraints
on the expansion and overpopulation of the major cities
have been one of the most important inducements to business to expand in the under-utilized development centers,
perhaps as important as government's financial assistance.

New York City may not be ready to accept limits on its
economic expansion, but it may well question its ability to
absorb additional rural migrants. All of the employment
trends in New York City—the relatively slow pace of
growth in the total number of jobs, the importance of white-
collar service occupations filled by women, the large number of low-paid, low-status, manufacturing and service jobs
—point to increasing difficulties in providing suitable employment for the existing population and its natural increment. If all of the large American cities in this same situation were to enact strict housing occupancy regulations, and
if they were to close substandard units, the nation might
be forced to cope with this national problem of misdirected
or undirected migration.

Certainly New York City is entitled to request federal
programs to facilitate the greater dispersion of Puerto
Rican migrants. Time might take care of this, as it has in

the great history of American immigration, but time is precisely what the metropolis does not have. In this connection, the French resettlement of its Algerian repatriates and West Germany's absorption of refugees from the East are examples of successful dispersion of migrants through national efforts.

Since the natural growth of the existing population is a cause for concern in terms of future employment opportunities, the city should make freely available to the poor and the minority groups all of the information and facilities for birth control which the educated and more prosperous citizenry already use. Freedom lies in knowledge and choice, not in ignorance and hardship.

Even if future strains on the city's capacity to provide sufficient employment are somewhat checked by one or more of the various measures discussed above, New York City may still have an excessive number of unemployed who might be placed if they receive proper guidance and training, and, in some cases, assistance with child care. It is important that the most employable persons be trained and offered jobs first, since employers in general are not willing to accept workers who are much below the current labor market standard.

Any hope that a large number of suitable new jobs can be brought into the city by inducing or subsidizing manufacturers to locate here seems vain and contrary to all long-run indications of New York's employment directions. Of course, New York City should encourage and remove the obstacles to the establishment or expansion of enterprise and employment, but it is doubtful whether considerable money, energy, or hope should be expended on trying to attract manufacturing firms which do not themselves seek to locate in the city.

A better alternative use of subsidy funds would be to assist workers to commute to available jobs in, say, Nassau or Suffolk counties, or to establish cheap transportation to selected employment points in the metropolitan ring, or to enable those who can find employment outside of the city to relocate permanently. Since New York City wants to raise the average income of its residents, one of the fastest ways is to export some of those at the bottom of the income distribution. This is a perfectly acceptable procedure if those who are aided or induced to go elsewhere can thus improve their own circumstances. Again, New York City by itself is capable of only limited action.

Efforts to train, re-train, upgrade, and improve the utilization of the entire labor force can redound to the benefit of those at the bottom of the scale. In the experience of the most advanced European countries, the single most effective method of creating vacancies for the hard-to-employ has been an overall program to improve the quality and productivity of those already employed, particularly by anticipating and acting on changing labor requirements. Until New York City can broaden its focus and administrative apparatus to provide an active manpower policy for the entire labor force of the metropolis, it will fail to uncover all of the possible jobs which might be filled by the unemployed or underemployed who need merely guidance and training.

Special job creation in community and public service activities to employ those who are considered employable but cannot be placed in competitive labor markets would be in the best tradition of Scandinavia, the Netherlands, and West Germany. A successful program entails at a minimum: the selection of socially useful projects which otherwise might not be undertaken at all, a sufficient and flexible volume of jobs to employ the majority of eligibles at any one time, and a built-in system of transfers to competitive employment. West Germany's program of job creation in the 1950s, when unemployment was high, is worthy of study.

If New York City can make an effective dent in its accumulated and projected overpopulation, underemployment, and unemployment, as suggested above, it may arrive at a position where comprehensive and permanent programs for the truly hard-to-employ can be established to replace present token actions. The single most important lesson to be learned from the European programs for this residual group is that a substantial portion will not find jobs in the competitive labor market and they can work only if jobs are created for them under sheltered conditions. If they are placed in such work, they should be encouraged to move to competitive jobs but not made to feel shame if they fail. Unless the New York City labor market becomes much tighter than it has been, the proportion of the labor force which needs the creation of sheltered jobs will be even higher than it has been in Europe.

Private employers should not be expected to provide much employment in such fields as low-income housing or to hire the hard-to-employ on such a scale that the problem can be solved. In Western Europe, the government stands ready to fill the gaps left by the private sector. Cooperation from local government, private and nonprofit organizations and employers, buttresses central government programs, which are the source of finance, administration, and planning.

It is important that any program for the hard-to-employ be adequate to the size of the group. This is not an area for a crash program or a demonstration project. It needs a continuing, permanent program, adequately financed and staffed. An enlarged and improved Employment Service is an essential prerequisite to effective services for the hard-to-employ. Specialists to identify this part of the labor market and to interview them in depth are a recognized need, as ordinary interviewers are too busy to perform this function. In Denmark, labor market specialists who know employers' needs and advise on placement give the hard-to-employ special aid beyond that offered to ordinary applicants.

The establishment of intimate working relations between the Employment Service and medical, psychiatric, social work, corrective, educational, and other agencies is highly desirable. It permits the manpower agency to accept referrals of hard-to-employ workers, since the screening and preparatory work have been done. And it allows the manpower agency to refer back for supportive services those who come to it with such serious problems that preparation for employment cannot be considered until remedial treatment has been given. In a country which has a comprehensive medical and social service, a high rate of seeking and accepting services and advice among the citizens, and good coordination between the manpower agency and other services, it is possible to keep the flow mostly in one direction —toward the manpower agency. This is a distant but desirable goal for New York City.

Among the most useful permanent institutions which can assist in the ultimate placement of the hard-to-employ are the work assessment and work training units, called Industrial Rehabilitation Units (IRU) by the British. Here, in a work setting, with time clocks, subcontracts from industry, duplications of business offices and situations, etc., it is possible to conduct psychological and vocational testing, counseling, assessment of work capacity, basic remedial education on a limited scale, training in work habits, and work experience which stresses accuracy and tempo. The IRU is not a substitute for ordinary occupational training or retraining or for sheltered workshops. Graduates of the IRU often are sent on for training courses and less frequently to sheltered work, since pre-selection should weed out those who are not candidates for competitive employment.

European experience does not encourage much reliance upon subsidized on-the-job training or employment for the hard-to-employ. However, considerable success has been achieved by trainees in government centers or facilities of nonprofit agencies, when the trainees have good work attitudes, are trained in shortage areas, and the training is of a high standard. For example, West German formal apprenticeship and training courses in prisons are widely accepted because the graduates take the same proficiency tests and acquire the same certificates as those outside the prison.

Among the requirements of a successful training program for the hard-to-employ who are slated for placement in competitive employment are: selection of the most employable, balance between trainees and known vacancies, adequate training allowances, variable course lengths to suit individual needs, and the opportunity for advanced training or education. Some countries separate the hard-to-employ from others in training courses.

It is assumed that most of the hard-to-employ wish to

work and welcome assistance to overcome their handicaps. But a number of cases have been noted where a disinclination to work is the primary obstacle to placement. The methods used to encourage work in Western Europe are persuasion, threats, and actual stoppage of unemployment insurance, assistance or welfare payments where suitable work is refused, and special psychological and vocational rehabilitation for the relatively few hard-core cases such as come before the British National Assistance Board. In Europe, suitable jobs include dishwashing and other menial, dead-end occupations at much less than $1.75 an hour.

It has been suggested that in Britain national assistance payments still enable a small group of single men to exist on a very low standard with few spells of work. No group on assistance comparable to the American mothers with dependent children can be found in Europe, but nowhere do such women lose their welfare payments if they do not take a job. Women outside of the labor force, whatever their marital or maternal situation, are not regarded as hard-to-employ.

The European experience suggests that a comprehensive large-scale program for the hard-to-employ, with considerable provision for job creation, is the only type worth launching. It is best started when general unemployment is very low and it should include: outreach, intake, testing, counseling, basic education, prevocational training, work experience, occupational training, job development, placement, and follow-up. Supportive services for health, education, social work, transportation, and day care of children are usually needed. Overhead functions include administration, research, program planning, and evaluation.

European programs do not appear to cost as much as

American programs after allowance is made for price and wage levels. Moreover, their results are more likely to be presented in terms of accomplishments than expenditures. Administrative overexpansion, leakages, and misuse of funds are very rare. There are secrets here that need to be learned.

In this review of the relevance of Western European labor market programs for New York City's accumulation of unemployment and underemployment, attention has centered first on ways of countering the excessive in-migration of rural, unskilled, poorly educated people; second on means of training and placing the unemployed employables; and finally on methods of helping the hard-to-employ to become productive.

But, in the last analysis, the details of specific European programs are less important than the underlying attitudes. The Western Europeans place a very high value on work, and they so greatly prize full employment, rigidly defined, that they have been relatively tolerant of price rises. All types of manpower are regarded as a scarce and valuable resource. The individual's inability to negotiate his way unaided through the complexities of the world of work requires that government smooth the way. In general, a large role for government and economic and social planning are approved. Finally, the enthusiasm for economic growth is tempered by a readiness to anticipate and cope with the social dislocations and costs attendant on economic change.

It is a very real question whether Americans can successfully transpose from Western Europe the specific ideas and programs for labor market adjustment on an adequate scale without a greater adherence to their basic values.

Part Three

Potential and Policy

9

The Potential of Educated Women

WHILE scores of urban residents are begging for jobs, many jobs go begging. This paradox is the result of the mismatch between the skills that rural migrants to the city can offer to local employers and the skills these employers seek. Since there is little likelihood of developing large numbers of unskilled jobs at a time when job requirements are rising, upgrading of the unemployed and underemployed is of critical importance. However, there are unfilled positions requiring high orders of professional or technical competence that are beyond the reach of persons with limited educational preparation. Although many of these shortages exist in areas of vital concern to the conservation of the city as a viable community, all sources of qualified manpower have not been fully exploited. Perhaps the foremost of these untapped pools of talent consists of highly educated women.

Large numbers of women who are presently precluded from employment are qualified to fill many urban job openings requiring high academic achievement. Among them are welfare workers and health professionals who are needed to serve disadvantaged residents. There are teachers and other educational specialists who are sought by city schools. There are holders of doctoral degrees who are capable of filling faculty vacancies in expanding metropolitan

colleges and universities. There are scientists and social scientists who can perform research and technical functions
essential to the operation of an increasing number of nonprofit and business organizations. These are but a few examples of the diverse talents that lie dormant waiting to be
used by a metropolis in need.

Although much attention has been paid to the immigration of highly skilled foreign technical and professional personnel to the United States, little if any note has been given
to a significant domestic brain drain—the exodus of highly
trained women from the labor market. All types of communities throughout the country suffer a loss of trained womanpower, but it is particularly costly to urban areas which
have special need for their skills.

The foreigner who has been seduced by attractive American employment opportunities simply transfers his expertise to a different environment. The woman who leaves
high-level employment, on the other hand, generally does
so to fulfill family responsibilities. And while the foreign experts usually expect their estrangement from their home-
land to be permanent, highly educated women are likely to
anticipate that their retirement from work is temporary,
since the more education women have, the greater is their
attachment to work. Prolonged preparation for careers and
the stimulation of satisfying work experience motivate
many women to continue their ties to their fields whatever
their circumstances and inspire others to seek to resume
their work roles as soon as possible.

If cities are to solve their pressing manpower problems,
they would do well to take account of the female brain-
power that would be at their disposal if efforts were made to
encourage its utilization and to accommodate to its needs.

There are many reasons for what is a fairly recent phenomenon on the American scene—the highly educated middle-class working wife. It is not the fact of advanced education alone that explains this situation, because women have long had access to college and university training. It has more to do with changes in social attitudes and in family planning.

Since the large influx of women into the labor force during World War II, the American community has become reconciled to the working wife and mother, although this dual role is not universally approved. This has had particular significance for women with the highest qualifications. While less-educated women find many personal satisfactions in work, the routine nature of the jobs for which most of them are qualified often influences those with no urgent need for additional income to stay at home. The highly trained woman, on the other hand, finds considerable self-fulfillment when her employment corresponds to her abilities. And she no longer has to contend with community disapproval if she chooses to remain in or to enter work that fits her capacities.

Where her status formerly demanded the surrender of personal aspirations to family goals, she now is able to work and still fulfill her family obligations satisfactorily. Thus, in ever increasing numbers, educated wives and mothers have joined their single classmates in the labor market.

Of course, even more than her neighbors' sanction, a wife needs her husband's approval. For educated women this is generally forthcoming, since they have educated husbands who tend to sympathize with their ambitions to test their skills in the marketplace. Therefore their husbands frequently cooperate with them by assuming a share of

home responsibilities and by giving preference to job locations that offer their wives greater employment opportunities.

But even if their husbands approve, most mothers do not
feel they can work when their children are young. And it is
in the sphere of family planning that the major changes
have occurred which offer women greater freedom of
choice between career and homemaking than ever before.
Girls are marrying at younger ages, including those who are
pursuing higher studies, and they are having children earlier.
Furthermore, the availability and use of birth control methods have enabled families to exercise control over both the
number and spacing of their children. A woman can limit
the size of her family and thereby shorten the period during
which child care responsibilities require her full attention.
Since the more children a woman has, the more time she
tends to spend at home, smaller families at younger ages
permit early reentry into the labor market. Most women
have their last child by the age of thirty-five. Although
highly educated women tend to marry somewhat later than
other women, they tend to have smaller families, which
means that retirement from work may be comparatively
short.

Yet while educated women are more likely to be in the
labor force than other women, there still are a large number
who want to return to work but who cannot find jobs because of barriers that prevent the utilization of their talents
in paid employment. This is a personal loss in terms of un-
fulfilled potential as well as a loss to society of essential
skills. While affluent America may be willing and able to
absorb the cost of extensive education that is never fully utilized, not all of the beneficiaries are equally complacent.

Many women regard the occupational success of some of their contemporaries with envy. Large numbers whose children are no longer at home contemplate the long years stretching before them with apprehension. Others consider the volunteer activities in which they might engage as inconsequential. Fewer and fewer of these women are content to settle for the personal satisfaction that accompanies learning and for the narrow application of their knowledge in the family arena or as community volunteers. Since many of the skills in shortest supply among active members of the urban labor force are those at top levels, it behooves all who are interested in relieving the shortage to consider the attributes of the educated woman who is ready and eager to return to work. She is available; she is trained and likely to be experienced; she has long years of work ahead of her; once hired, she is a stable and creditable employee.

It might be supposed that, given a pool of trained women who are eager to put their training to use and employers who need their skills, it would be a simple matter to match the two. However, this is not the case. Many women are unable to work because conditions conducive to their employment do not exist. These conditions vary with individual circumstances but they are of two general types: those that constrain them from seeking employment and those that prevent them from obtaining employment. Among the first group are problems connected with child care, vocational guidance, additional education, and costs incidental to working. Those that limit placement possibilities include discriminatory employment policies, anti-nepotism regulations, and inflexible work schedules.

The insistence upon the continuing presence of the mother throughout a child's early years is beginning to lose its force as a result of the many studies that indicate that not only can child care be delegated to others if the parent-child relationship is secure and stable but that young children may gain when their mothers are able to derive satisfactions from both within and outside the home. Thus, many mothers of young children have fewer compunctions about combining home and career responsibilities than in the past. The major hindrance to employment is the unavailability of child care assistance.

The multi-generation household rarely exists today, and mothers can no longer rely on relatives to care for home and children while they work outside. In many instances, the grandmother herself is working. Other mother substitutes are scarce. Many former domestics now find factory, office, and sales jobs available and preferable to tedious and solitary household employment, even where pay is comparable.

There have been suggestions that an upgrading of domestic work through special training courses, particularly of that aspect concerned with child care, might develop a supply of mother substitutes from among both young high-school graduates and older women with limited interest or background in commercial fields. Programs for mother's aides might attract the same type of students as those who currently undertake preparation as nurse's or teacher's aides. If conditions of work for graduates of such a course were closely controlled and supervised, perhaps by public and private domestic employment contractors, a satisfying image of the paid mother's substitute might obliterate the hitherto demeaning implications of domestic service.

However, even if it were thus feasible to supply care for infants and very young children, a mother substitute in the home is not necessarily the desideratum for preschool children of working mothers. The popularity of the nursery school attests to the desirability of giving young children opportunities for socialization and for early learning experiences. They also provide working and nonworking mothers with free time for personal or career pursuits.

Private nursery schools and many public facilities generally operate on a half-day basis and, although this may satisfy a mother who can find a position that allows her to work during school hours only, it does not meet the needs of full-time workers or of women working on part-time schedules that are not restricted to the school period. The proliferation of nursery schools and the establishment of the Headstart program suggest that the community has recognized that preschool children derive substantial benefit from organized study and play opportunities. It is probable that, like the kindergartens which were originally privately sponsored experimental undertakings before they were institutionalized within the school organization, the pre-kindergarten may become an accepted adjunct to the educational system. In the meantime, cities that wish to encourage the employment of highly trained women will find it to their advantage to promote the establishment of all-day child-care facilities to serve working mothers at all levels of competence and income.

Another problem the educated woman faces when she decides to return to work is how to proceed in her search for employment. Women who have been away from work for long periods of time are handicapped in seeking career guidance.

The young woman with a new degree has the advantage of recent training which she plans to put to immediate use.

The returnee is frequently unsure of the current market value of her educational attainments and earlier work experience. She needs aid in evaluating her employment potential and in obtaining a position. Because she is uncertain about her worth as an employee, she often hesitates to seek the work she wants.

Most placement agencies and personnel offices are directed toward the employment of individuals with specific job interests. Few are ready or able to provide counseling for those who are uncertain about the type of work to seek. Those organizations which are prepared to advise and guide the returning woman worker are few in number and are not well known.

Cities should make special efforts to improve and publicize existing guidance and placement services for qualified female manpower and, if necessary, to establish new specialized facilities for this purpose.

Most women with graduate degrees are likely to be eligible for employment on the basis of their education and earlier experience without pursuing additional studies. However, some women, for a variety of reasons, may wish to undertake further education. Women with bachelor's or first professional degrees may want to enter doctoral programs; professional women may wish to be trained in a field of specialization; women with degrees in liberal arts may want to qualify for schoolteaching; some women may wish to shift from their original field. Others, whose fields have changed markedly since their retirement, want to familiarize themselves with new developments before seeking employment.

Many of these women, particularly those who are interested in pursuing programs of graduate or professional studies, find it difficult to be admitted to universities. Discrimination exists with respect to both young would-be graduate students and to older women interested in additional study.

To the younger woman, the usual rationale given for the preferential treatment of male applicants is the expectation of career discontinuity for females. However, it is prima facie evidence of discrimination when the primary basis of selection of degree candidates is other than individual ability. Moreover, it demonstrates insensitivity to the preference of many educated women for continuous work patterns for all or most of their lives. To exclude able women from advanced education solely on the erroneous assumption that their training will be wasted is unjustifiable and an academic contribution to the waste of human potential.

Older women find even less receptivity within universities than younger ones if they wish to pursue graduate or professional education, except in "feminine" fields. Since most admissions to graduate training are provisional, there seems little reason to deny this opportunity to older women with the necessary prerequisites. There is evidence that older women who have been admitted to advanced programs are satisfactory and often superior students. If enrollments are limited it is understandable when younger applicants with longer continuous work-life expectations are given preference. But the need for increased professional and technical manpower should persuade universities to give consideration to expansion of opportunities for graduate study.

In addition, if the rigid time requirements of many courses of graduate and professional study were relaxed, many women would not have to abandon their educational goals completely while engaged in homemaking. They could pursue studies at their convenience and, if necessary, progress from part-time to full-time education when circumstances permit. Most opportunities for modified study schedules are on the undergraduate level, but there is a demand for graduate courses as well that would allow women to proceed much faster into the work world when ready. Since many graduate programs provide opportunities for extensive individual study and research, it is often only the inflexibility of traditional academic practices that prevents the wider introduction of part-time arrangements. The self-interest of urban institutions of higher learning dictates that they should train personnel who can be utilized in their own expanding educational undertakings as well as in the surrounding community.

Perhaps one caveat is in order with respect to continuing education. Recent projects to provide education or training in new fields to older women are laudable, but further study is not necessarily a prerequisite for those with graduate degrees who wish to resume interrupted careers. Too many women hesitate to offer their services to employers after a hiatus at home without embarking on additional education to enhance their job prospects. However, many job openings exist in fields where techniques mastered in earlier graduate education and work are likely to be durable enough to withstand a period of disuse. Social work, teaching, medical and research skills, for example, can often be immediately reapplied, particularly when, as is frequently the case, contact with one's field has been maintained through reading, meetings, and even through volunteer activity. Employers will often find that a minimal period of on-the-job practice enables returnees to refresh and to update their skills and knowledge. Counselors, employers, educa-

tors, and returnees should be made aware that continuing
education is designed to do what has been left undone, not
what may be redundant.

Another major deterrent to the entrance of married
women into the labor market has been the high costs incidental to work. Primary among these are the costs of child
care. A woman may find that her salary, particularly a
starting one or a part-time one, fails to cover all expenses
concomitant to work or leaves her with minimal net returns, and she may be thereby deterred from continuing her
career after childbirth or from pursuing it later. Some husbands are willing and able to subsidize their wives' work by
shouldering the added expenses, but this is a burden which
cannot be assumed by all of them.

If qualified women are to be encouraged to perform
work that is socially and economically beneficial, society
must begin to consider tax adjustments for working women
who hire domestics. A cultural lag exists between fiscal policies that constrain women to remain unemployed and social attitudes that look with favor upon their employment.

Although significant tax reforms must take place on the
state or federal levels, local governments can assist women
who want to work by providing free facilities for child care
or by subsidies for that purpose. Private employers, too,
might find such costs to be worthwhile in terms of benefits
derived from the continuing employment of highly qualified
women employees as well as from the reentrance of equally
able women. At the least, it would be desirable for urban
employers of the highly educated to use their influence to
press for tax reforms that would redound to the benefit of
wives and mothers who wish to combine home and career.

All of the hindrances to a continuation or resumption of

a career do not involve personal circumstances such as domestic help, guidance needs, educational preparation, or family finances. Many women are ready, willing, and able to seek employment but cannot find jobs because of discriminatory employment practices or rigid scheduling policies.

Title VII of the Civil Rights Act prohibits discrimination in employment on the basis of sex but its coverage is limited, and many of the positions sought by highly trained women are not affected by its provisions. Moreover, it is characteristic of antidiscriminatory regulations that proof of intent to discriminate is difficult to obtain.

Discriminatory practices vary from field to field but even in the so-called "feminine" occupations, prejudice often exists with respect to supervisory and administrative positions. And in some employing organizations, women at upper echelons tend to be a last resort if they are resorted to at all.

The Civil Service has been relatively free of discriminatory practices and is a significant employer of well-trained women. Business and academic institutions, on the other hand, have been notoriously discriminatory. The most pressing manpower needs of urban business firms are likely to be in technical areas which are generally open to women. It is largely in managerial assignments that businesses discriminate against women (except, possibly, in retailing) primarily because of the influence of unrealistic stereotypes of the female executive. Yet experience in working atmospheres conducive to feminine achievement suggests that where women are encouraged to perform on high administrative levels, their performance and achievement are comparable to those of men.

However, from the standpoint of urban manpower needs

and female interests and aptitudes, discrimination against women by colleges and universities is much more significant and even harder to rationalize. Not only do women face prejudicial hiring policies in the academic world but they are also subject to bias in the assignment of rank, tenure, and responsibility. It is paradoxical indeed that institutions which are willing, albeit sometimes reluctantly, to train women to serve on college faculties, are the same ones that avoid hiring them except on temporary or auxiliary bases.

Furthermore, colleges and universities are among the most flagrant practitioners of anti-nepotism; many have express or implied rules against the hiring of two members of a family as permanent staff members, especially if they are in the same academic discipline. Since many educated women marry men in their field, this practice often denies them an opportunity to work in their field.

Wives can sometimes solve this problem by working in another institution in a metropolitan area. But such a choice is not always available and, if it is, the varying strengths of schools may mean that a faculty wife must settle for second best if her husband's employer is the preferred employer.

Since intensive efforts are being made to prepare urban youth for higher education and to provide increased opportunities for them to pursue college studies, faculty recruitment is of the utmost importance. Antediluvian discrimination against women, in general, and against faculty wives in particular, hampers procurement of adequate staff members. Not only are qualified women often prevented from the maximum exercise of their talents, but many of their husbands decline offers of faculty positions when satisfactory opportunities are denied their wives.

Urban universities perform direct service for the city in

terms of educational and research contributions, and they are also extremely important in maintaining a city's cultural and intellectual preeminence. Individuals of intellectual distinction have been attracted to cities by their distinguished halls of learning and, in turn, their achievements have contributed to the image of the city as a brain center as well as a nerve center. If the city is to continue to serve as a magnet for students and scholars, public and private urban institutions of higher learning must reexamine policies that may be repelling the very individuals they wish to attract.

There is an additional form of employer discrimination based upon age. Often the older returnee is arbitrarily rejected. We certainly would not deny the young woman an opportunity to start upon a career, particularly if optimal conditions exist to foster a continuous work pattern after marriage and motherhood. But while the newly trained woman has the advantage of recent formal education, the returnee can often counter this with maturity and seriousness of purpose. Too often younger women look upon early work experience as a time-filler until marriage. The returning older woman has achieved this goal and is prepared to direct her energies toward achievement in her chosen career.

Another limitation upon female employment is the unwillingness of many employers to hire women on less than a full-time basis. For some educated women, the chance to engage in part-time work allows them to maintain continuous ties to their fields after marriage and childbirth. For others, it permits an earlier return to work when home duties have diminished but still require some of their time. In both cases, part-time work not only satisfies a woman's desire to work in her career field but also provides her with

easier access to full-time employment when she feels ready
to increase her working hours. Although an increasing
number of women work part time, some of whom have no
intention of becoming full-time workers, many women with
professional or technical training consider part-time work a
temporary resolution of the problem of combining work
and home activities.

However, many of these women experience difficulty in
finding positions which permit modified work schedules.
Many employers, public and private, have been reluctant to
hire part-time personnel, particularly those with high degrees of competence, despite growing evidence that there
are few if any jobs that cannot be performed on a part-time
basis. Not only do such occupations as teaching, medicine,
social work, library work, and research easily lend themselves to flexible hours, but some increasingly important
types of technical work, such as systems analysis, are
equally susceptible to part-time arrangements. The organizational changes that are required to accommodate to flexible scheduling are minor when the gains that can result
from the utilization of highly motivated and skilled employees are considered.

One has only to recall changes in the average work week
over the last generation to realize that most full-time workers today are employed for a period that would have been
formerly classified as part-time, and there is the increasing
possibility that future full-time work will be performed on
even shorter schedules. Although top-level personnel tend
to invest more time in their work, this is more likely to be
the result of individual than managerial needs. Where work
can be carried on in a separate compartment and does not
require frequent communication and interaction among

staff, part-time employment seems particularly suitable. School and college teaching, medicine and dentistry, accounting, counseling, among other fields, are of this character. There is also reason to believe that for the same pay level, part-time workers give a higher hourly output than full-time staff.

Rather than suffer from personnel shortages because of insistence on full-time schedules, business and government might find it highly beneficial to restudy their personnel needs in the light of the availability of women who can work only part-time and who otherwise meet their requirements.

If all barriers encountered by women desirous of entering the work force were removed, the question of their availability would still arise because large numbers live at a distance from urban employment opportunities. The flight of the middle class from the central city has been a much-discussed and often deplored phenomenon. But, for large numbers of the middle class, the city exerts strong pulls. Particularly among the highly educated, an urban environment is the sine qua non of a life of continued cultural and intellectual exploration and enrichment.

Few commuters are able to partake readily of the city's varied diet of leisure-time activities, of the excitement and stimulation of being spectators, and often participants, in meaningful events. Although many outlying areas are trying to emulate the metropolis, the aura of the city, although tarnished in many respects, still overshadows the copies.

But even the most dedicated city dwellers often find that the disadvantages of urban living outweigh its advantages. Problems of schooling, housing, and neighborhood deterioration lead many reluctantly to remove themselves to suburbia. This, in itself, may be grounds for a woman's decision to leave work.

Although cities may never be able to match some suburban attractions, they may be able to retain more middle-class residents if intensive efforts are made to provide desirable schools, homes, and surroundings. Environmental improvements may help to stay the emigration of city residents, and they will attract back to the city suburban residents whose parental responsibilities are fulfilled. As a result, fewer educated women will find it necessary to abandon careers in order to move out of the city and more middle-aged females will be conveniently located to participate in the urban labor force.

If city employers wish to fill those vacant professional, technical, and administrative positions that can be of significant aid in restoring the health of the metropolis, they should initiate, encourage, and reinforce the following policies to stimulate the employment of educated women.

Expanded child-care facilities should be provided and located near workplaces as well as in residential neighborhoods. If city governments are reluctant to subsidize women workers who have more than a minimum income by providing their children with free preschool accommodations, voluntary centers serving all working mothers could be organized with public support for children who need it and a sliding fee schedule for others. Such operations would be similar to that of the voluntary hospital and could give preference, where necessary, to children of mothers who work out of financial necessity and to those whose mothers are performing essential services in the community. Women from both groups can be recruited to serve as professional or auxiliary personnel in these projects.

Colleges and universities should establish similar facilities for mothers who are students or staff members. These should also be open to neighborhood children. Such facilities can also be used as demonstration projects for students.

An experimental program to train mother's aides should be developed as part of a vocational school curriculum, as an adult education venture, or both. Consideration should be given to supervised employment of trained aides, perhaps on a contractual basis. Publicity about the program should stress the special competences taught, attractive employment conditions, and a reevaluation of homemaking services, in order to encourage participation.

Assistance for educated women who wish to resume careers must be more readily available. Guidance and placement services presently offered by public, community, and private agencies must receive greater publicity through such media as alumnae communications, organs of volunteer organizations, public service advertisements, magazine articles, and radio and television presentations. College and university counseling and placement offices should be encouraged to make their services available to alumnae. Since women seeking help in returning to work are likely to be interested in immediate employment, counseling services should provide placement assistance as well as guidance. It is essential that the work aspirations of the temporarily retired woman not be frustrated because of lack of acquaintance with career opportunities. The establishment and strengthening of guidance services both within the city and in peripheral communities will permit her to embark on her search for meaningful work as soon as the spirit moves her.

Closely connected with the foregoing is the necessity for

an expansion of educational opportunities for both able female college graduates who wish to pursue higher studies and older women with advanced degrees who wish to refresh their knowledge of their fields, to undertake additional training, or to venture into new careers. Since city governments have a large stake in the expansion of the supply of highly trained personnel, they should insure that publicly sponsored universities offer equal considerations to all qualified applicants. Private urban institutions should follow suit since it is also in their interest to provide assistance in filling manpower needs that will stem local deterioration and attract students who will learn and live in the metropolis.

Part-time graduate and professional study should be more generally available to women who would like to combine their schooling while meeting family responsibilities.

Consideration should be given by urban universities and foundations to the establishment of programs for independent study, similar to the Radcliffe Institute, where highly qualified women receive financial aid in meeting family and other responsibilities while they engage in graduate study or research.

Many factors enter into a consideration of subsidization or tax allowances to cover child-care arrangements for working mothers. Such questions as eligibility, family income, and occupational status have a bearing on the feasibility of compensating highly skilled women for the costs they incur by working. Since society makes a substantial investment in the education of these women, it would seem to be socially and economically advantageous to encourage the exercise of their talents in the community, particularly when many of these are in short supply. As a beginning, it might be worth comparing costs and benefits of various methods of subsidy and tax relief to determine whether private and/or governmental action could be effective in maintaining and stimulating the working capacity of qualified women.

Discriminatory employment practices in upper occupational echelons are more difficult to check than are those affecting less-skilled workers. Although legislation prohibiting discrimination on the basis of sex exists, there are subtle means by which employers demonstrate bias against females that circumvent the intent of such laws. Women should be encouraged to seek redress if they believe they have been subject to prejudicial action by employers. Organizations that typically place barriers in the way of feminine achievement should be urged to review their policies. Sex qualifications should be eliminated from recruitment literature, from "Help Wanted" advertisements, and from job orders to placement agencies.

Guidance and placement agencies should encourage the employment of older women by informing employers of the successful integration of older women into a variety of enterprises. Consideration should also be given to the establishment of flexible retirement policies which would enable women who reenter careers in their late thirties or early forties to continue working as long as they are capable of being productive.

Many employers provide intensive on-the-job technical and managerial training programs for young women with college and graduate degrees who, after a few years, terminate their employment to undertake family responsibilities. This particularly characterizes areas of substantial importance to the urban economy, such as systems analysis, retailing, accounting, and finance. If employers proceed upon the assumption that most of these women will eventually wish to resume their careers, they might find it worthwhile in terms of savings in recruitment and training costs to maintain contact with females in temporary retirement. News letters, periodic meetings, and refresher courses can serve as inspiration and preparation for a return to former positions. By maintaining contact with former female employees, these firms would have a pool of experienced potential workers who can meet high-skill requirements without undergoing intensive indoctrination.

In this connection, a review of policies relating to maternity leave is in order. Provisions permitting absence for childbirth should be broad enough to allow for variations in the length of time during which a mother remains at home without prejudice to her reemployment, particularly in areas of skill shortage where these women's talents are at a premium.

The existence of urban employment opportunities for women with advanced training can be of substantial benefit to city employers desirous of recruiting male personnel. For many men, willingness to relocate is influenced by the vocational needs of their wives. It may be desirable, therefore, for employers to familiarize themselves with local job openings that might appeal to the wives of these men and even to stimulate the development of such opportunities.

It is equally desirable that these employers review anti-nepotism regulations which may hinder both the optimal exercise of women's competencies and the recruitment of male experts whose wives are summarily excluded from employment at the same organization simply by virtue of their relationship.

Employers in all sectors should review their policies with respect to part-time employment. City governments should give immediate consideration to stimulating the establishment of openings for part-time employees in such areas as teaching, social work, and health, where the demand for skilled womanpower is great. Business and nonprofit employers might also gain from flexible time-schedules which will place many highly trained women at their disposal. Where there are shortages of full-time personnel, it makes more sense to consider the employment of part-time workers than to suffer the disabilities of inadequate staffing. In this respect women may well be in the vanguard of the moves toward further reduction in working hours, as employers find that certain functions can be performed as efficiently and productively on shortened schedules.

Finally, city government, which is interested in serving the unmet needs of the community, in increasing the supply of professional, technical, and managerial skills for present and potential employers, and in attracting and retaining middle-class residents, should initiate a study of female labor resources in the metropolitan area with the goals of identifying its special characteristics and of determining its employability. Once this is accomplished, an intensive effort should be made to provide the conditions necessary to encourage employment. There is too much confusion on the part of employers, government, training institutions, and vocational advisers about the role of the educated woman. But there is little confusion on the part of the women themselves. Although they have wide options, almost uniformly they demonstrate a close attachment to the world of work. They also tend to be attracted to the diversity and stimulation of urban living. If they are encouraged to respond to urban opportunities for the satisfaction of their career needs and are further spurred by environmental improvements, the city will gain essential workers and desirable residents.

10

Higher Education

THE present chapter is an inquiry into the manpower aspects of higher education in New York City, and the policies of the City of New York with respect to higher education in terms of their effect on manpower in the city.

The significance of higher education to an economy has long been in the forefront of every discussion of educational functions, planning, and support. Only within the last decade, however, has it begun to receive serious and continuing examination as an important area of manpower and economic policy. So far, the subject has been systematically approached largely as a matter of national policy. Once we consider the question from the point of view of a smaller part of the national economy, it takes on new dimensions. Educational planners in the South and West have studied the problem, but a systematic approach to higher educational planning in relatively small areas has not yet been undertaken in parts of the country which are leaders both educationally and economically.

With a system of free higher education and an extensive system of private colleges and universities with schools, departments, faculty, and students of the highest quality, the city has long taken its system of higher education for granted. However, as the economy grows and changes, and as economic development efforts at the state and local level become increasingly important, it is necessary to deliberately approach the question of how the city can maximize its position via the institutions of higher education in it.

New York City is perhaps the only major city where questions of manpower planning in relation to higher education can be faced in their full complexity. It is the only major city which operates its own system of higher education. In most other cities, the public university system is under the aegis of the state. Other major cities have a concern similar to that of New York City, but it has not been considered a matter of urban planning policy.

A derivative of the lack of concern with higher education in this or any other city is the paucity of useful data relating to higher education and the city. Most data are collected at the state level or by the U.S. Office of Education and aggregated on a state-by-state basis. Without useful data, it is difficult to make definite comments. Therefore, the following discussion will attempt to lay out the connections between manpower policy and institutions of higher education and to suggest special aspects which relate to the city. As such, the following discussion becomes an agenda for serious thought and research.

New York, Higher Education, and Manpower

There are several manpower aspects of higher education in New York City. First, access to higher education has significance to individual citizens, since it directly affects their career and income-earning potential. Second, institutions of higher education are economic enterprises which provide services to the larger community and for which they are paid by individuals, by governments, or in other ways. These revenues provide the means to employ individuals and purchase goods and services from other enterprises and institutions and thus create employment. Directly or indirectly, institutions of higher education are responsible for a significant and growing amount of employment in the city.

Third, higher education contributes to the growth of the local economy and economic enterprises through the development and training of high quality manpower, the generation and dissemination of ideas, and in other ways. By affecting the economic structure and particular enterprises and sectors within it, the institutions of higher education have a profound and quite general effect on employment patterns and manpower policies throughout the city.

The institutions of higher education in New York City are in a unique position in that the city itself is a national center for many different facets of the economy, government, culture, and society. New York City is the major city of the United States, and indeed of the world, and it acts as a headquarters for national and international businesses, finance, banking, insurance, and legal affairs. It is the center for publishing, communications, television, radio, business services, and advertising. Its theater, artists, museums, and entertainment centers influence the arts, culture, and popular entertainment throughout the world, and are an integral part of New York as a center for tourism and conventions. It is one of the world's centers for medical treatment as well as for medical, scientific, and social research. It is a major center for the philanthropic foundations and business and trade associations. New York City is the urban center, *par excellence,* and serves as a model for educational, social welfare, human rights, planning, renewal, and

other social welfare programs. Finally, New York is the
home of international government and the center of a growing effort at regional and intergovernmental operations involving local, state, and federal governments.

The fact that New York City is a center for so many activities provides its institutions of higher education with
unique opportunities for instruction and research, although
the expanding universities have not always capitalized on
these opportunities. The opportunities for close association
with institutional developments in these various worlds, as
well as for immediate, supplementary, or later employment,
have always been a major factor in attracting to New York
faculty and students in such fields as English, history, lan-
guages, economics, and business. New York's position has
also led to a rapid expansion in international studies in the
last two decades, ranging from studies of foreign areas to
specific inquiries into the government, history, and culture
of other regions and countries as well as into international
business and economics. There have been, in addition,
efforts to build educationally on New York's position in
communications, entertainment, theater, and the arts. The
major universities of the area have cooperated in the establishment of a Center for Urban Education, although its
major emphasis to date has been on education below the
college level.

Basically, a symbiotic relationship exists between New
York City and its institutions of higher education. The city
provides powerful assistance in developing instructional
and research materials. Universities in the city can be influ-
ential as these graduates move into the centers of power
and influence. This, or course, makes the city all the more
attractive to faculty, researchers, and students. In turn,

those in power and influence rely on the institutions of higher education to provide them with trained manpower and ideas. Those who are employed in central activities also rely heavily on local universities for a diversity of continuing educational opportunities to shore up weaknesses, to continue fundamental development, and to keep abreast of changes.

Colleges and universities of the city are concerned with the development of people who go on to employment in a wide range of local public and private activities, including teaching, social work, business, accounting, law, and the like. Indeed, the city's institutions of higher education probably have more of an effect on the regular functions of the city than as leaders in national and international affairs. This is simply because of the sheer numbers of college-educated persons involved in the normal activities of the community. Through them, the colleges and universities have a profound impact on the effectiveness and productivity of the city's entire economy and society.

Functions of Institutions of Higher Education

The services provided by colleges and universities are undergoing significant transitions, and it is necessary to understand each of them and their interrelationships if effective policies are to be developed. The traditional and still primary role is that of instruction. Increasingly, however, even this role is changing. Graduate and professional education steadily increases in importance as does post–high-school occupational education. Part-time and evening education continues to increase in importance.

The importance of study past the traditional ages for col-

lege attendance is also growing. In part, this reflects the increase in part-time attendance in traditional degree programs. In part, it represents part-time attendance of an avo-
cational nature. There is, moreover, a sizable and probably
increasing number of students in their thirties, forties, fif-
ties, and even sixties who are returning to liberal arts, professional, and graduate study either to increase their personal and occupational competences, to enter a profession
for the first time, or to enter a second profession. Finally,
the importance of a range of *ad hoc* educational devices is
increasing, including special institutes, conferences, lecture
series, and the like. These devices serve to broaden hori-
zons, teach new techniques and findings relevant to a profession, or overcome weaknesses or add competences as the
individual, the organization employing him, or the field in
which he works develops.

Even more important than transitions in the types of students and instruction is the rapid growth in noninstruc-
tional functions. Particularly in connection with graduate
and professional studies, there has been a great growth of
research operations, sometimes within the regular departments of instruction but often in special institutes and
projects. Much of this growth has been financed by the federal government, and originally was heavily defense-
oriented and in the physical sciences. Increasingly, however,
federal funds for research have gone into the medical, bio-
logical, and social sciences and into service-oriented activities in health, education, welfare, urban life, and the like.
One-half of the budget of Columbia University now comes
from federal contracts. Federal funds have long gone past
the point of providing supplementary salaries for faculty
members, and now pay for large numbers of full-time pro-

fessional, technical, clerical, and other personnel, an increasing proportion of university overhead, and an increasing proportion of capital expenditures for buildings and equipment.

Colleges and universities are also increasingly involved in providing other services for students, faculty, and employees. Urban universities find that more and more students want to live on or near the campus even if their parents live in the area. Faculty housing and parking create new or expanded demands on the university or college. Provisions for dining, shopping, and medical service are growing. Printing, publishing, and reproduction services are also expanding. Each institution confronts these problems differently and deals with or attempts to ignore them in different ways, but all are affected.

Finally, in the course of instructing, developing, and otherwise serving their students, institutions of higher education frequently begin to conduct a number of activities which provide services to the surrounding community. For instance, budding physicians, nurses, social workers, teachers, and other professional workers must learn to some extent on the job. This can be either in a service institution or agency operated by the university, or in one in which arrangements for supervised learning experiences have been made. Once involved in running a teaching hospital, or say, a demonstration school, the university tends to serve a broader section of the community. Finally various service activities may be provided simply because they are needed and it seems convenient for the university to operate them.

It also happens that a university, willy-nilly, operates as a service institution for the community, as when its campus is used as a park, its libraries and halls are used as resting places and day-time shelter by the tired, old, and cold, and its lunchrooms and incidental shopping facilities are frequented by the indigent and others seeking low-cost meals and goods.

In the final analysis, a vast array of services is offered to the surrounding community by the university because it must meet students' needs for instructional and developmental experiences, because it feels a community obligation, because it is compassionate, because it cannot feasibly limit their use, or because any additional funds are welcome. Among this vast array of services, moreover, will be teaching hospitals, demonstration schools and projects, vocational advisory services, student citizenship projects, cafeterias and lunchrooms, lecture series, movies, sports stadia, park and sports areas, neighborhood sports programs, police protection, and others.

The Structure of Higher Education in the City

New York City has a great number of institutions of higher education, but most of the activity is concentrated in a few systems or institutions. Enrollments provide a convenient way to illustrate this point. As Table 9 indicates, there are thirteen colleges and separate institutions with a total of over 148,000 students within the public sector. Four senior colleges in the City University account for 109,000 of those students.

Within the private sector, there are more than 170,000 students. However, 66,000 are in two institutions, and 51,000 are in the next largest four. The remainder—over

Table 9.   Enrollment in Colleges and Universities in New York City, 1965 and 1966

	1966 Total	1965 Total	1965 Degree Credit	1965 Full Time
PUBLIC INSTITUTIONS				
City University of New York				
University Programs	4,034	643	643	259
Senior Colleges				
City College	30,482	29,912	29,912	12,407
Brooklyn College	27,839	24,875	22,874	10,787
Hunter College	27,006	26,136	26,136	10,146
Queens College	23,952	22,464	22,032	10,469
Community colleges				
New York City Community College	10,064	9,347	1,162	199
Bronx Community College	7,049	6,648	2,824	1,398
Queensborough Community College	4,242	3,660	1,756	1,021
Borough of Manhattan Community College	2,838	1,695	610	279
Staten Island Community College	2,813	2,549	1,412	812
Kingsborough Community College	2,326	1,913	1,913	1,502
College of Police Science	n.a.	1,089	1,089	9
Total, C.U.N.Y.	142,645	130,931	112,363	50,288
Fashion Institute of Technology	4,944	4,552	—	—
State University of New York				
Downstate Medical Center	816	831	831	827
Total, public institutions	148,405	136,314	113,194	51,115

PRIVATE INSTITUTIONS				
New York University	40,711	31,825	31,156	14,831
Columbia University	25,227	25,124	25,066	14,645
Long Island University [a]	18,160	16,196	15,563	9,752
St. John's University	12,202	13,125	13,125	8,826
Fordham University	10,887	9,980	9,980	6,759
New School for Social Research	10,105	10,084	2,187	447
Pace College (Manhattan)	7,273	8,006	8,006	2,741
Yeshiva University	5,265	4,867	4,539	2,893
Polytechnic Institute of Brooklyn	5,094	5,622	5,622	1,972
Manhattan College	4,622	4,838	4,354	3,466
Pratt Institute	4,351	4,238	3,809	2,814
New York Institute of Technology	4,195	3,577	3,577	2,901
R.C.A. Institutes, Inc.	n.a.	3,522	1,202	934
Wagner College	2,633	2,589	2,589	1,835
St. Francis College	2,214	10,084	2,139	1,303
College of Insurance	n.a.	1,845	215	116
Brooklyn Law School	1,308	1,401	1,401	934
Cooper Union	1,280	1,314	1,314	802
Academy of Aeronautics	n.a.	1,322	1,322	1,035
Julliard School of Music	n.a.	1,021	1,021	723
College of Mt. St. Vincent	990	878	878	754
Parson's School of Design	n.a.	726	726	726
Bank Steet College of Education	711	694	694	111
St. Joseph's College for Women	694	714	714	639

Table 9 (continued)

		1965		
	1966 Total	Total	Degree Credit	Full Time
PRIVATE INSTITUTIONS (CONT.)				
Manhattan School of Music	n.a.	654	654	562
New York Medical College	583	575	575	575
Marymount Manhattan College	535	565	565	565
Union Theological Seminary	n.a.	553	553	485
Jewish Theological Seminary of America	n.a.	511	493	412
New York Law School	478	518	518	253
Notre Dame College of Staten Island	476	478	478	471
Mills College of Education	465	420	420	412
Finch College	375	300	300	299
Chiropractic Institute of N.Y.	n.a.	300	n.a.	n.a.
Voorhees Technical Institute	n.a.	268	n.a.	n.a.
New York College of Music	n.a.	260	260	190
Cathedral College of the Immaculate Conception	n.a.	234	234	234
General Theological Seminary	n.a.	192	192	180
Atlantic States Chiropractic Institute	n.a.	180	n.a.	n.a.
Mannes College of Music	n.a.	176	176	147
M. J. Lewi College of Podiatry	157	133	133	133
Rockefeller University	129	118	118	118
Junior College of Packer Collegiate Institute	n.a.	115	115	115

Biblical Seminary in N.Y.	n.a.	86	86	54
Columbia Institute of Chiropractic	n.a.	78	n.a.	n.a.
College of the Holy Names	n.a.	60	33	26
Duchesne Residence School	n.a.	57	n.a.	n.a.
Passionist Monastic Seminary	n.a.	31	31	31
St. Charles Seminary	n.a.	14	14	14
Hebrew Union College: Jewish Institute of Religion	n.a.	n.a.	n.a.	n.a.
Total, Private Institutions [b]	*161,120*	*162,523*	*147,147*	*87,235*
Total, All Institutions [b]	*309,525*	*298,837*	*260,341*	*138,350*

[a] Total enrollments, a significant proportion of which is located outside New York City.
[b] Not comparable.

50,000—are in forty-eight separate institutions. Many of the smaller schools are highly specialized in religious studies, the minor health professions, music, education, and the like.

The great majority of the students in New York are in degree programs or taking courses which can be credited toward degrees. While there has been a sizable growth of community colleges and technical institutes in recent years, only about 23,000 in the public institutions and less than 17,000 in private institutions are in programs which cannot be credited toward a degree.

Part-time education is of vast proportions. In public institutions, over 62,000, or more than half the students taking degree credit courses, are part-time students. In private institutions, the numbers and proportions are smaller, less than 50,000 or just over 35 percent are part-time students.

Finally, the institutions of higher education in New York City are more heavily oriented toward graduate study than is general throughout the country. The data suggest that New York City accounts for about 5 percent of all undergraduate students in the United States, but for nearly 9 percent of all graduate students. Indeed about 1 in 8 women in graduate work in the United States studies in New York City. These women are studying primarily at the master's level, which undoubtedly reflects the value of a master's degree for schoolteachers.

Higher Education for the City's Citizens

Perhaps the city's primary manpower concern with institutions of higher education is the development of skills and income potential of the city's citizens, particularly the oncoming generation. It would be helpful if we could trace the preparation of the citizens of the city for college, their attendance at, and employment subsequent to, college and graduate study. We need a complete flow analysis. Unfortunately, the data are not available.

In recent years, 78 percent of total enrollments in grades nine through twelve in New York City have been in the public schools. Approximately 60 percent of those leaving public high schools have a diploma. Although the proportion with academic diplomas has declined somewhat, about 60 percent of all graduates make application to a post-secondary institution, and nearly all of them attend. We do not know however how many private- and parochial-school graduates attend college.

Despite our emphasis on local universities, we must not overlook the fact that college and university students, highly educated persons, and information and ideas are highly mobile. Data for 1963 show that 87,833 New York City undergraduate students were attending colleges full time within the state. Of these, 73,491 were at schools within the city, and 13,333 had gone to the suburbs or other parts of the state. On the other hand, 14,332 students, primarily from the suburbs, were going to college in the city. Thus, the city had a small net gain of students from the rest of the state. We do not know how the universities in the city fared with respect to the interstate migration of students, but New York State as a whole tends to send many more undergraduate students to other states than it receives, and receives substantially more graduate students from other states than it sends. We can conclude that the city exports more undergraduate students than it receives, and that it receives more graduate students than it sends to other parts of the country.

Educational planning is ordinarily directed at the development of young people through full-time study. Over the decades, however, part-time studies and the education of persons somewhat older than the conventional student have grown so that they merit a more central place in planning. At New York University, for instance, 24,000 out of 41,000 students are part time. Two-thirds of these part-time students are men. About 8,000 are in the School of Continuing Education, but the remaining 16,000 are in the regular departments and schools. The major concentration, some 12,000, are in the various graduate schools, especially education, business, arts and sciences, and engineering. However, some 3,000 are in various undergraduate colleges and schools, and about 1,000 are in the professional schools. There are some part-time students in almost every school and department. Large numbers of part-time students are in almost all the larger universities of the city, and the subject patterns are roughly as above.

In the graduate and professional schools of New York University, nearly 20 percent of all students and 5 percent of all full-time students are over thirty-five years of age. At Columbia, over 10 percent of all students in the graduate and professional schools and above 5 percent of the full-time students are over thirty-five years of age.

The New School for Social Research has long attracted older students, but they tend to be relatively less common in the other universities of the city. In general, older full-time students tend to be in education, social work, library service, the social sciences, and the humanities. In these fields, it is not unusual for them to comprise 20 percent or more of all students. Very few older students are found in engineering, physics, chemistry, and mathematics.

Meeting Manpower Needs in the City

The second principal manpower effect of local colleges and universities which interests the city is their role in supplying the manpower needs of the city's public and private economy. This subject has received periodic attention at the national and state level, but little at the city level. Nationally, the vast majority of college and university trained people are employed by government either directly or indirectly, i.e., in privately producing goods and services for sale to the government. Most of this is a matter of federal contracts, but the employment of teachers, social workers, administrators, and others by local government is a highly significant factor.

From the point of view of the city, therefore, the demand for college- and university-trained personnel for the local economy might be broken down into the following parts, not necessarily in order of priority: manpower for the city's operations, manpower for federal and state operations, manpower for goods and services produced locally for sale to the city government, manpower for goods and services produced locally for sale to the federal and state government, and manpower for local employment in the private sector.

Each of these sectors of demand has its own occupational characteristics, but only fragmentary estimates exist about them. Thus, no general comments can be made as to how well demands for highly educated manpower in the city are being met. In general, one would expect that the ability of the city to attract, retain, and contribute to the growth of private industry, governmental operations, and governmental contracts would depend in part on the availability of highly trained manpower. However, the importance of this factor varies greatly from industry to industry, and little of a specific nature can be said at this point.

In this connection, the availability and quality of local facilities for continuing education sometimes play a key role in the location of industrial facilities. For engineers, for instance, where skill obsolescence is a particular problem, continuing study is important either to refurbish one's skills or to prepare to move into a management position. This opportunity often plays a role in the selection of locations for various operations.

Import and Export of Brain Power

As noted earlier, college and university students, highly educated persons, and information and ideas are highly mobile. Educational opportunities for the citizens of the city are the source of highly trained manpower for the local economy and cannot be discussed in isolation.

In the first place, New York may attract a greater or lesser number of students from abroad, from the rest of the nation, from the suburbs, or from within the city. Students from within the city may study abroad, in other parts of the state or the United States, or within the city.

The self-interest of the city with respect to these flows needs examination. For decades, for instance, the City of New York educated without charge many of its own citizens, regardless of income. One recent report states that less than 5 percent of the City University's students are from outside the city. The New York City population has also relied heavily on local private colleges, professional schools, and graduate schools. Even those with national and international standing have always had high proportions of city residents among their student bodies. At the same time, great numbers of students from the city have gone to private colleges and universities in the Northeast and to public universities in the Midwest. The growing publicly operated system in New York State may attract increasing numbers of city students, but a 1965 report stated that only 4 percent of the State University's students were from New York City.

On the other hand, the city's private schools and colleges are increasingly drawing students from the growing suburbs. Private universities are increasingly involved in educating a growing number of foreign students, although their position with respect to students from the rest of the state and the United States remains to be defined.

The graduates of local colleges and universities are primarily employed by local industry and institutions, but many go elsewhere in the country and abroad. Similarly, the local economy attracts persons trained in the rest of the country and abroad. Some of these were New Yorkers in the first place, but others are attracted to the city after they finish their education. Finally, it should be noted that there is a constant stream of educated people into and out of the city at various stages of their lives, depending on the exigencies of careers and personal affairs.

Without comprehensive statistics, it is difficult to foresee the city's future position with respect to the attraction and losses of highly educated manpower developed locally or elsewhere. One survey of graduates of City College showed that about 2 in every 3 holding degrees in business and education and over half of those with degrees in arts and sci-

ences live in the city. However, less than half of the graduates of the School of Technology had remained in the city.
Between 13 and 21 percent of the graduates lived in the
suburbs. The percentages who lived outside the metropolitan area ranged from 14 percent for business graduates to
18 percent in education, 27 percent in the arts and sciences,
and 36 percent in technology. In general, men were more
likely than women to be located outside the city or metropolitan area. Those in their thirties were more likely than
those who were younger or older to be located outside the
city and metropolitan area.

In general, we can say that a strong and thriving local
economy tends to import highly trained manpower at every
level—as college students, as graduate students, as graduates entering employment, and as experienced personnel.
New York City seems to violate this generality at several
points. This may represent a weakness in so far as the future growth and economic health of the city is concerned.

Higher Education as an Industry

Higher education is becoming a significant industry in the
United States. Institutions of higher education are sizable
markets since they need goods and services to carry on their
operations. The general expenditures of the private universities in New York City were estimated at more than $140
million in 1966 by the State Board of Regents. The same
year the City University of New York reported educational
and general expenditures of $108 million. Nearly $6 million more passed through auxiliary enterprises. Thus a total
of $250 million is now being expended for current pur-
poses, and the amount is increasing rapidly. In addition, be-

cause they are rapidly expanding, universities have been and continue to be heavily engaged in construction. In 1966, the City University had capital fund expenditures of $19.2 million. Even so, this total is no more than 1 percent of personal income generated inside the city, which has been running at much more than $30 billion per year.

As with most service enterprises, most of the current expenditures of institutions of higher education go for the services of professional and other manpower. Roughly 145,000 people are employed by the educational institutions of the city.

The occupational mix of the city's institutions of higher education is suggested by data on twenty-six private and nonprofit educational establishments holding government contracts reported in a recent survey by the Federal Equal Employment Opportunity Commission.

These data, which cover over 19,000 persons, are useful even though they are not fully representative, since they include only about 1 in 8 employees in higher education in the city, only 1 in 4 employees of private universities and colleges, only 1 of the 2 major private universities, and nearly 1,000 persons from other types of educational institutions.

As Table 10 indicates, approximately 42 percent of the employees of these private institutions of higher education were in teaching or other professional posts, 6 percent were in managerial work, 11 percent were technicians, and 23 percent were in clerical positions. Service workers comprised more than half of the 18 percent in blue-collar jobs.

No estimates have been prepared of the employment effects of the purchases made by universities and colleges in the city. Presumably, they are significant for construction

employment. The private universities have begun to contract-out much of their operations in connection with food
service, local security, parking, and the like. This pattern
probably will increase in the future, and may include cleaning, dormitory operation, and other aspects of university
operation.

Table 10. Occupational Distribution and Minority Employment in 26 Private Educational Service Establishments, New
York City, 1966

	Percent Distribution	Percent Who Were:	
		Negro	Puerto-Rican
Professional	42.1	2.8	1.5
Officials and managers	5.6	5.0	1.4
Technicians	11.3	15.0	4.6
Sales workers	0.1	16.7	8.3
Clerical	23.1	14.2	6.8
Total, white collar	82.2	7.9	3.4
Skilled	1.6	12.3	5.2
Semiskilled	3.3	11.9	11.4
Laborers	1.6	34.2	26.8
Service workers	11.3	44.2	19.1
Total, blue collar	17.8	35.8	17.0
Total Employment	100.0	12.7	5.9

Other Manpower Effects

Because of their position as public institutions, community
leaders, and shapers of community values, the employment
policies of institutions of higher education with respect to
members of minority groups are of particular concern. Because of their numbers and generally depressed conditions,
Negroes and Puerto Ricans are the center of concern at the

present time. As Table 10 indicates, Negroes comprise about 13 percent and Puerto Ricans 6 percent of the employees of private institutions of higher education in the city. This is a slightly higher proportion than prevails among other private employers and it obtains in spite of the fact that universities and colleges are so heavily oriented toward professional level personnel among whom minority groups tend to be scarce.

As a matter of fact, these minority groups are relatively more important in each of the various occupations in the institutions of higher education than in private employment. Even so, half of the Negro and Puerto Rican employees of the universities and colleges are employed as service and other blue-collar workers. This is a significant fact, nevertheless, since universities and colleges are one of the few expanding sectors of the economy which employ sizable numbers of relatively unskilled persons, who encounter the greatest difficulty in finding jobs.

The institutions of higher education in a city have significance for the economy of the city in other ways. The trained manpower employed in a university are often also employed by other public, private, or nonprofit organizations. Professors, particularly, may be employed either on a regular basis in a consultant capacity, or for specific periods of time. This work is usually on a paid basis, but public and nonprofit agencies often employ professors without a fee. Sharing of personnel is encouraged by many factors: 1) many persons in universities have relatively scarce talents and skills; 2) non-university organizations often do not need full-time permanent employees with certain skills; 3) university personnel, particularly faculty, are usually not employed full-time in their basic functions; 4) university personnel traditionally enjoy considerable leeway in adjusting their schedules at the university, including class schedules, and they have vacations during the school year, long summer vacations, sabbaticals, and opportunities to reduce their schedules or take an unpaid leave; 5) it is often to the advantage of university personnel to serve in other organizations, since they are thus exposed to situations and ideas which enrich their teaching, research, and other university functions; and 6) university personnel moving among or working simultaneously with a variety of non-university organizations often serve as an effective conduit for ideas and information.

In this connection, we should note that universities also are enriched by the utilization of non-university personnel on a part-time or intermittent basis (paid or unpaid), as teachers, researchers, consultants, conference participants, or other sorts of advice and information givers. Thus, the university shares in a variety of ways scarce but highly valuable skilled and talented people in a modern community. These opportunities have reciprocal advantages to the private organizations, not the least of which is that opportunities to work in and around a university provide considerable satisfaction to many professional and managerial personnel and perhaps incidental income. For these reasons, university opportunities are often an important factor in the attraction and retention of valuable and even key personnel by public and private enterprises.

The long-run manpower effects for a city of the institutions of higher education have another dimension. Many people who start out in one sector of the economy either choose to or are forced to change their career orientation in middle age. Thus, university personnel may leave for a second career in private or public employment and thus provide a valuable manpower input for the latter. Conversely, a certain number of privately or governmentally employed professionals and managers undertake academic careers in middle age, or as they retire from their first employment, which may be relatively early.

It is useful to make a distinction between the way in which universities share and transfer manpower and skills and the way they share and transfer information. The latter has been one of the traditional functions of the university; the former is just beginning to become important. It is doubtful that the sharing and transfer of manpower is actually new. However, it is more and more important because of the increasing size of the educational establishment and the increased extent to which the natural and social sciences and various professional disciplines are utilized in and are relevant to private and public enterprises.

Although it is traditional for universities to be engaged in the development, analysis, and dissemination of ideas and information, the growth of research operations in recent years means that they are increasingly important for the metropolitan area in which they are located. Information and ideas begin to flow to the outside community long before they are formally published or disseminated. Those who are geographically close have some advantages in terms of the early transmission of ideas and information. Similar advantages exist in the case of preliminary papers, draft materials, and even the final publications. Newspapers, local journals, local professional associations, and the like all share in this transmission at the local level.

Key Policy Questions

Just how funds are allocated within an educational system represents important manpower policy decisions. It has been estimated, for instance, that $100 million of the $160 million annual expenditures of the City University go for liberal arts and science programs, $50 million for explicitly career-oriented programs, and $10 million for administration. This reflects the strong tradition within the system to emphasize liberal rather than occupational education. It also represents the conviction that liberal education is economically productive in the long run, perhaps even more than occupational education.

In a certain sense, the policy control of institutions of higher education has been slipping out of the hands of the normally responsible persons, whether the Board of Higher Education or the boards of trustees of the private universities. This is because the sources of funds are slipping from local government, tuition, and philanthropy, to state and, increasingly, national governments. Whoever pays the piper tends to call the tune. However, in a system of responsibility or of pluralistic control, the recipients of funds can often exercise considerable control through the political process, administrative procedures, and their own force of will. Their efforts to retain or extend control are likely to depend on how well the recipients know what they want. This makes it all the more necessary for the city to consider carefully and in detail just how it can be aided or hindered by various developments in the city's public and private universities and colleges.

There is a growing tension between the city and the suburban areas with respect to the institutions of higher education in the city. In part this is reflected in and due to the different legal positions, traditions, and financing of public higher education in the city and upstate. In part, it reflects the shift to the suburbs of the traditional market for the services of these institutions, i.e., the emergent and established middle class. In part, it also reflects the struggle for adequate space for expansion.

The institutions in the city enjoy many advantages in this struggle over and above simply being there first. As the center of so many worlds, the city has greater attractions for many students and faculty. Whether they can more readily serve the rising number of persons seeking incidental, part-time, and even full-time education through middle age may well be a critical question in the future. Clearly, the city enjoys advantages over the suburbs in the attraction of students from the rest of the country and abroad.

The problem of space is critical for universities. The very essence of a university is shared facilities, faculties, ideas, and students. For this reason, a real university tends to concentrate in one geographic location. Institutions which are divided experience a continuing set of conflicts and problems.

Most universities which emerged after the turn of the century, and especially since the 1920s, are surrounded by deteriorating neighborhoods. Thus, they are constantly acquiring real estate in the surrounding neighborhood, which is used first as an investment and hedge against the future, and later to house marginal or new operations of the university. Finally, the buildings are razed to make way for new facilities.

The question of space illustrates that universities and colleges relate to the city much as does any private industry. Universities and colleges have problems with space, local transportation, traffic, parking, local security, and the rest. Whether or not these problems are solved has a bearing on the growth and retention of higher education, just as they do for industry, and thus on the degree of local prosperity. The growth and retention of higher education has added importance because it affects the quality of manpower for the city's economy at large.

Another crucial question in the expansion of higher education is its relation to the expanding program of federally sponsored research and development. These programs are significant not only for the development of new knowledge, but also for the attraction and retention of faculty and students. This is particularly important in the graduate and professional schools, but it affects undergraduate schools as well. Paradoxically, schools which emphasize teaching to the virtual exclusion of other activities may find that the quality of their teaching has declined because they cannot get the necessary faculty nor can their faculties keep easily abreast of changes in their fields.

New York City faces the problem of the growth of higher education in a much more direct way than do other cities, precisely because it and its educational sector are big and diverse enough to make policy decisions difficult, and also because they can pay off well. Because the city is so big, it can directly benefit from a strengthening of its educational establishment. A small city can increase its attractiveness as an educational center but, again precisely because of its size, it will be prone to lose educated manpower to other centers either initially or as individuals pursue their careers. New York City is so large that professionals employed in law, medicine, architecture, business, economics, writing, the arts, and many other fields can profitably spend their whole careers in one or a series of organizations in the metropolitan area. Since New York City is inevitably the hub of the megalopolis which extends from Boston to Newport News, the attractiveness and critical importance of New York City as a focal point for career ladders which cut across diverse organizations, including the federal service, become obvious.

The question of balance among the various universities and colleges is constantly open. Each institution tends to be unique, for each has different strengths and weaknesses. Each tries to meet certain types of needs in the community. Each attracts and selects certain types of students. Only in the broadest sense and only along certain lines are institutions in direct competition with one another.

Over time, however, new educational needs develop and the strengths and weaknesses of different institutions begin to change. As a result, the contours of the various institutions and the competitive boundaries between them evolve and shift. This is largely a process of complementary adjustments. Policy shifts on the part of the leading institutions tend to create opportunities for policy shifts and complementary adjustments for others. Columbia University's shift to emphasize full-time graduate studies some years back created the opportunity for other institutions to grow through increased part-time enrollments. As New York University attempts to emphasize academic quality, deemphasize its service function, improve the quality of its undergraduate and graduate students, and limit part-time enrollments, this will create opportunities for expansion by other institutions. To the extent that the demands for grad-

uate studies are growing, the establishment and growth of
the City University graduate programs may have little effect
on other institutions. Difficulties and perhaps retrenchment
on the part of some private institutions would create the
demand for expansion of others.

The quality of the faculties of the total higher educational complex in the city is worth some concern. While educational planners have dealt in various ways with the expansion of the total educational system and its parts in
terms of institutions, buildings, and curricula, the continuing development of their faculties has received relatively little concern. One expects graduate faculties to be self-
improving, for they are the source of new ideas and of
research findings. College and professional faculties associated with them are stimulated in turn. There may be a serious question of the continuing growth and development of
the faculty members in other institutions. While many of
these individuals study, write, and carry out research on
their own, they and others may suffer from their relative
isolation. Just as many employers and leaders of professions
are concerned with continuing education and development
of their professional manpower, there is reason to be concerned about the continuing development of college faculties. The possibility of new forms of institutional relationships may assume greater importance in the future. The
Center for Urban Education represents one attempt to provide a framework for the support and encouragement of research and study by faculty members in diverse institutions.
University seminars at Columbia University have always included members from its own faculties, the faculties of
other universities, and interested professionals employed
outside the university. There may be room for other forms

of research associateships for faculty members in secondary universities and colleges in the various research programs and institutes in the leading universities or in other kinds of cooperative ventures.

This chapter has laid out in broad strokes the connections between manpower in the city, the institutions of higher education, and the policies of the city. The principal thrust has been to suggest the scope of an analysis so that research, data, and the development of appropriate policies can proceed hand-in-hand.

11

Public Policy for Growth

THIS chapter will attempt to provide the outlines of a growth strategy for New York City in the years ahead. Because the emphasis will be on strategy rather than on comprehensive planning, it will seek to identify those few key factors which, on the one hand, can provide maximum leverage for expanding employment opportunities, and which, on the other hand, stand as critical stumbling blocks to the future growth of the city. By concentrating on a few key factors, it is hoped that the many alternatives confronting New York City's political leadership can be reduced to a comprehensible and manageable few.

Before outlining a growth strategy, we must deal with several antecedent issues which, because of the accountability of the New York City government to its electorate, have important political implications. The first of these is the relationship between jobs and economic growth. Should municipal officials concentrate on increasing employment opportunities and hope that in this manner the city will be able to grow economically? Or should they concentrate on stimulating the economic growth of the city, measured in per capita income, hoping that as a result new employment opportunities will emerge? There is more of a distinction here than might at first appear, since it may be possible to

increase employment opportunities without raising per capita income or without providing any net addition to the
number of jobs available within the city. Political pressure
arises because certain segments of the electorate are concerned primarily about increasing employment opportunities—particularly employment opportunities for which
they can qualify.

The growth strategy outlined below is predicated on the
assumption that it is not only preferable but essential that
the political leadership of New York City set itself the goal
of stimulating maximum economic growth, ignoring except
as a secondary consideration the objective of increasing
employment opportunities particularly for certain socioeconomic groups. There are several reasons for insisting on
this order of priorities. The first is that an emphasis on increasing employment opportunities for particular socioeconomic groups may well lead to policies inimical to the city's
long-run growth. Resources, including the energies of the
city's political leadership, are limited, and their use for one
purpose often precludes their use for another. An honest
sympathy for groups which need additional employment
opportunities might dictate some sacrifice of economic
growth in order to provide additional jobs were it not for
the fact that the long-run interest of those very groups lies
precisely in maximizing the city's economic growth. This re-
lates to the second reason for subordinating the goal of increasing employment opportunities.

In discussions of the city's minority problems, it is sometimes argued that municipal officials should concentrate on
attracting industries which employ primarily unskilled or
semiskilled labor, since these are the industries likely to
provide job opportunities for those who need them most.

However, this view overlooks the fact that even an industry employing primarily skilled and semiprofessional workers also requires a proportion of unskilled and semiskilled help. From the point of view of the unskilled and semiskilled, the ideal industry is one which, by providing a natural career progression, offers them the prospect of eventually moving up to a skilled or semiprofessional status. The above view also ignores the fact that it is a growing industry which makes available the maximum number of job opportunities, not an industry which is barely holding its own—and most of the industries employing primarily unskilled or semi-skilled labor are of the latter sort. Finally this view, if systematically pursued as municipal policy, would probably doom those socioeconomic groups whom it is intended to benefit to the same types of low-paying jobs which they now find so frustrating and disheartening.

The proper emphasis for the city's manpower program is the training and building-up of skills for better jobs in the future, not the wooing of industries to meet the present imbalances in the labor market. Given the city's lack of voice in determining national economic policy, it can work most effectively from the supply side rather than from the demand side of the labor market. To the extent that individuals are more highly skilled, and thereby have greater vocational and geographical mobility, they will be better able to protect themselves in that market.

The ability of the city to provide those municipal services which are the prerequisite for skill acquisition will depend on the growth of its economy. The greater that growth, the larger will be the social surplus that can be tapped through taxation and the more plentiful will be the funds to finance education, medical care, and other forms of investment in human beings. So far New York has escaped the fate of some cities which, because of inadequate tax sources, cannot provide the level of municipal services necessary to assure continuing growth and, because of insufficient economic growth, are confronted by a shrinking tax base. But there are signs that New York City may be on the brink of a downward spiral, and the subordination of the goal of economic growth to other objectives could give it the final push.

The second antecedent issue involves the relationship of New York City's economy to that of the metropolitan area as a whole. Should municipal officials be concerned only about the level of per capita income and/or the number of jobs within the five boroughs, or should they determine their policies from a larger perspective? On this issue, political pressures virtually dictate the former. Those who vote in municipal elections are likely to care only about what happens within the city itself, and its ability to influence developments outside the city's borders is very slight. Nevertheless, the growth strategy outlined below is predicated on the assumption that only by viewing New York City's economy as part of a larger regional economy is it possible to plan meaningfully for the future.

New York City as a separate entity lacks the land resources to meet the needs of those economic activities which give it a comparative advantage over other metropolitan centers. It must therefore be able to draw on the land resources of the surrounding region to maintain its own vitality. This requires, of course, that there be some means of coordinating decisions affecting land usage by the various political subdivisions. More will be said on this point.

The various parts of the region—particularly, New York

City and its environs—are important to each other in two
ways. They are an important source of demand for each
other's services, which permits more efficient production of
those services, and they are an important source to each
other of the productive inputs which they, separately, lack
in sufficient quantities. From this perspective, a decision by
a particular business firm to move part of its operations
from the central business district in Manhattan to a nearby
suburban community is hardly reason for concern by municipal officials. By expanding into the suburbs where land
is more easily obtainable, the firm may be spared the need
to move all of its operations, including the executive offices,
out of the metropolitan region. (It is the retention of the executive offices in Manhattan's central business district
which will be most critical to New York City's economic future.) At the same time, valuable space in the central business district is freed for other economic activities. Moreover, the location of the firm's facility in the nearby suburbs
will add to the overall demand for the specialized services
which New York City offers to the surrounding region. In
all ways, then, the city may be better off.

It can thus be seen why a growth strategy for the City of
New York in isolation makes little sense. Put another way,
effective economic planning for New York City can be undertaken only from a regional point of view, with recognition for the specialized role of each part of the region. The
validity of this proposition will become clearer when the dynamics of regional growth have been set forth.

The rate of economic growth for a region such as the
New York metropolitan area, which is highly developed but
not self-sufficient, will depend primarily on the ability of
that region to finance the importing of the goods and ser-

vices which it lacks through the exporting of goods and services to other regions. Of course, a certain amount of growth can be generated simply through an increase in population, as additional economic activity is required to meet the needs of larger numbers of people. Moreover, such growth can also come about as a result of climatic, demographic, social, or political factors unrelated to economic developments. Finally, as the per capita income of a region increases, the types of goods and services which its population demands may change to those less dependent on the resources of other regions, and thus the region becomes more self-sufficient. Even when all these qualifications are noted, however, the crucial importance of the region's export sector—those industries enjoying a market beyond the region's borders—is still evident.

A region is able to export goods and services to other regions—and overcome the obstacles imposed by transportation and communications costs—when it has comparative advantages in carrying out particular types of economic activity. Since a region's economic growth is dependent on its export sector, and the export sector in turn is dependent on the region's comparative advantages, the key to an optimal growth strategy for the region is the protecting and enhancing of its comparative advantages. What are New York City's comparative advantages, both at present and in the foreseeable future?

A listing of these advantages must begin with the city's unique transportation facilities centering around the Port of New York. This unrivaled harbor, with its nearly 800 miles of waterfront protected from the ocean yet open to ships the year round, was the initial source of New York's rise to pre-eminence among American cities. Together with the Erie

Canal, a system of regularly scheduled packet boats to Europe and a large fleet of intercoastal schooners, it made New York the favored point of entry for men and goods moving from the Old World to the New, and back again. By 1870, the Port was handling 57 percent of this country's foreign trade.

Since then, various factors—including the dispersion of population and economic activity, and shifts in the composition of foreign trade—have reduced the Port of New York's relative importance, although its absolute volume of trade has grown. Nevertheless, two recent developments promise to enable New York not only to hold its own against rival ports in the future but perhaps even to increase its relative position. These two developments are the trend toward the use of containers and the rapid growth of air freight. Together they open up the possibility of a transportation revolution which may, as one consequence, lead to the concentration of international commerce in a smaller number of port cities, thereby reversing recent trends in this regard. This is because it may again become most economical to consolidate shipments at a single point on this side of the Atlantic before beginning and after terminating the transoceanic leg of the trip.

Stimulating this transportation revolution and in turn being stimulated by it is the substantial increase in international trade which the United States is likely to experience in the years ahead. While the outlines of this development are not entirely clear (it must still be molded by future political and economic events), the favorable signs can be discerned. These include the rise of world income and the growing number of countries that are becoming part of an international money economy, the almost limitless need of the underdeveloped nations for capital goods imported from abroad, the superiority which the United States enjoys in the production of certain technologically advanced goods, and the previous relative neglect of foreign markets by American businessmen. This increase in foreign trade, if and when experienced, should make the Port of New York an even more dynamic factor in the future growth of the city—provided the region as a whole pursues wise policies.

The second comparative advantage which New York City has over other urban areas is its preeminence as a center of financial and business activity. Like the existence of the Port itself, from which it historically evolved, this "capital market" and "corporate headquarters" function gives rise to a series of external economies which tend to reinforce the city's position of predominance. Officials of many nationally important financial institutions and business firms, in order to be in daily contact with their counterparts in other companies, maintain offices in New York City. But other financial institutions and business firms have located in New York City for the same reason. (A similar set of forces has led to the concentration of nonprofit organizations in New York City, beginning with the need of these philanthropically supported groups to be near the center of wealth and financial management.) Moreover, the presence of so many large corporations in New York City, both financial and nonfinancial, makes possible the existence of numerous industries supplying special services to the business community. These industries encompass the Wall Street law firms, the Madison Avenue advertising agencies, the West Side printing establishments, and the Broadway theaters and nightclubs. Again, the fact that business service industries are so readily at hand adds a further incentive for large corporations to locate in the metropolitan area—if not in Manhattan's central business district itself.

The capital market and corporate headquarters function which New York City serves is directly tied to the state of the overall economy. As the level of national output continues to grow—and there is no reason to believe that it will not—so should this element in the specific economy of New York City. While certain staff activities may be forced, because of lack of space, to locate outside the city itself (though it is hoped within the region), the central decision-making groups should find that the most advantageous location is still in Manhattan's central business district south of 60th Street—provided, again, that the region as a whole pursues wise policies.

The third and last of New York City's comparative advantages lies in the complex of cultural and communications institutions which make the city preeminent in that regard as well. They include the resident companies of Lincoln Center, the other theater, music, and dance groups, the television and radio networks, the book and magazine publishers, the museums and libraries, the private art galleries, and the universities. While the city may not be first and foremost in every area, the range and quality of institutions, complementing and reinforcing one another, serves to make it the cultural and communications capital of the United States—perhaps of the world. The location of the United Nations on the East River is testimony to that preeminence, as well as an important source of economic activity in its own right.

New York's comparative advantage in this regard was due initially to the large number of persons with incomes sufficient to permit them to indulge their taste for the arts

—a derivative of the city's predominance as a financial and business center. But this factor was soon reinforced by the same type of consideration which induces many large companies to locate their central offices in Manhattan. Since the most opportunities in the cultural and communications fields are found in New York, it has attracted the most talented individuals. And since it also offers the largest pool of talented individuals, it is the best place to begin a new endeavor in one of these areas. Only when other considerations are overwhelming, such as was the weather for the movie industry, is New York apt to be bypassed in favor of another location.

As for the future, the increasingly higher levels of income which Americans will come to enjoy should make them ever more eager for the services which New York's cultural and communications institutions offer. While one effect of this greater demand will undoubtedly be the establishment of rival institutions in smaller urban centers throughout the country, just as the increase in foreign trade made possible the growth of rival ports offering the same full range of services, it should also assure that the cultural-communications complex remains a dynamic and growing factor in New York City's economy—again subject to the proviso that wise governmental policies are pursued.

As one final comment on New York City's comparative advantages, the extent to which each of the three major types depends on the others should be noted. New York, for example, would be less desirable as a port of entry if it did not have financial institutions ready and able to supply working capital for large importations. Again, it would be less desirable as a home of national and international corporations if it did not have ready access by jet airplane to other parts of the country and of the globe. Similarly, the cultural-communications complex, by providing after-work entertainment, makes the metropolitan area a more desirable place for business leaders to establish their central offices; while the same service industries which have arisen to meet the needs of the business community also underpin the successful functioning of the cultural and communications institutions. It is for this reason that New York's comparative advantages should be viewed as an organic whole. But while each is important to another, they do have differing needs. It is this fact which calls for specialization within the region.

New York City, and in particular its central business district, lacks one of the resources which is vital to the continued growth of the activities which, together, constitute its comparative advantage. That resource is space. How it is allocated, not only within the city but within the metropolitan region, will significantly determine the health and rate of expansion of New York's economy. This is a type of decision in which government must play a major role, not only because it is so crucial but because government is already so deeply involved. Indeed, if we had to identify a single critical factor on which New York's political leadership should focus its energies, that single factor would be the city's scarce and valuable land resources and their allocation to different economic functions. Thus the growth strategy this chapter has to offer is primarily a suggestion of the principles which should govern land usage in New York City and, inferentially, in the surrounding region as well.

In general, the city should allocate its valuable land resources to those economic activities which generate the highest regional value added per worker per square foot of space. (Value added is equal to the revenue received by each business firm, government agency, or nonprofit organization less its expenditures on materials. It is roughly the same as employee compensation and profits. Regional value added is that portion of total value added which accrues to individuals working in the New York metropolitan region. If regional value added is divided by the number of persons in the work force per square foot of space, the result is regional value added per square foot of space—or r.v.a., for short.) Consequently, the city should see that prospective users of land generate a certain minimum r.v.a. before they are allowed to occupy space in the city. This minimum r.v.a. should be higher for Manhattan's central business district than for other parts of New York City and higher for activities conducted primarily during the daytime than for those conducted primarily at night.

If this general principle governing land allocation is to prove useful, several qualifications must be kept in mind. The first is that when a particular activity, such as the overnight printing industry, is inextricably linked to some larger economic function, such as the capital market and corporate headquarters function, and cannot be located except in a certain part of the city without impairing that larger function, its claim on New York's land resources should be that of the larger economic function. This rule would mean that first priority would be given to those activities which contribute to the maintenance and growth of New York City's comparative advantages. For example, a new office building, housing the corporate headquarters of a large national company or an expansion of the facilities of the New York Public Library would have this prior claim. However, when a particular activity, even if part of some larger economic

York City has long had over other urban centers—and this has both strengthened and been strengthened by its other comparative advantages—was the quantity, quality, and diversity of its labor force. For example, no other city could have so well provided the cadres to man the offices of all the large financial institutions and other corporations that are located in New York. These workers are an important source of economic strength to the city and they must have a place to live—if not in New York City itself then in nearby communities easily accessible by commuter transportation. At one time, the four other boroughs alone were able to perform this bedroom function for Manhattan; now it must be performed more and more by communities outside the city's political jurisdiction, a fact which once again points up the need for a regional outlook in planning.

New York can assure itself of an adequate work force in one of two ways: either by making land available for residential purposes or by making the necessary investment in commuter transportation facilities. On the one hand, it seems clear that the city alone—even all five boroughs— can never provide enough sufficiently desirable housing for all of its work force. Some parts of the city already have a greater population density than is socially healthy, and if other parts of the city were to be exploited more fully as residential areas through the erection of high-rise apartment buildings, they would either be deserted by families with children or turned into vertical slums. On the other hand, it seems equally clear that the city cannot survive without providing some housing for its work force within its own boundaries—including even the central business district. Some persons are simply unwilling to commute long distances to work each day. More important, a city without a residential population with an economic interest in its survival and growth will be a city without the social and political leadership necessary to enable it to endure and thrive.

Whether to reside in the city close to the place of one's employment or to commute long distances each business day is essentially the economic decision of whether to trade convenience in getting to work for more living space. While this decision will depend primarily on personal preferences, it will in the aggregate be related to two factors: family size and income. Households with children have the greatest need for space, while households with large incomes will be best able to afford it. Thus the family with an annual income of $20,000 and no children will be more likely to live in Manhattan than the family with $10,000 a year and three children. From a knowledge of the family size and income of the work force, it should be possible to estimate the balance likely to be struck in the future between those who will want to live in the city itself and those who will prefer to commute from outside the city to their places of employment.

In undertaking such an analysis, however, it must be kept in mind that those members of the work force with the lowest income—particularly those who belong to the peripheral group described in another chapter—will present something of an economic anomaly. Rather than residing in the less-crowded areas either at the fringe of or outside the city, they are most likely to be found—regardless of family size—heavily concentrated in the core of the city. The reason for this housing pattern which flies in the face of economic rationality is that a certain minimum level of income is required to live outside New York City and commute daily to work. Members of the work force with the smallest incomes have no alternative but to remain in the city, and even there they are unable to command the space necessary for a comfortable existence. Thus, New York City, unlike many surrounding communities, tolerates the overcapacity utilization of its housing. This tendency of low-income members of the work force to be concentrated in an economically irrational manner at the core of New York City is, of course, accentuated when they are members of minority groups subject to discrimination in housing and thus unable, even when they can afford it, to move outside the ghetto areas.

It has been suggested that the solution to this problem requires the construction of more publicly owned or publicly subsidized housing. The fact remains, however, that whether assisted by government or not, the lowest income groups will, as long as they continue to reside in New York City, be put in the position of having to bid for the scarcest and therefore most costly space in the metropolitan region. Housing is, after all, only one of the many demands made on space; even if housing were provided without charge, low-income groups would still lack adequate space for other aspects of daily existence. Equally important, if the city were to attempt to meet all the needs of its low-income groups for housing and other living facilities, it would have land resources for little else. Provision of better housing would simply attract more low-skilled and thus more low-income workers to New York. It would not be long, however, before the city government would be confronted by a fiscal crisis, both because tax-yielding activities would be unable to expand for lack of space and because the publicly assisted housing programs would create a serious drain on the city's financial resources. For these reasons, public housing is unlikely to be more than a limited program.

This is not to argue that, as a limited program, public housing is undesirable, even though it constitutes a subsidy to the low-paying industries. New York, no matter how much the average skill level of its work force can be upgraded, will always have a sizable number of persons unable to afford decent housing; as a form of assistance to these individuals, public housing can help to maintain a healthy balance of socioeconomic groups within the city. It can also give a needed boost to the more upwardly mobile of the low-income workers during their early, lean years. This is merely to suggest that the saturation point for low-income public housing may have been reached—at least in Manhattan—and that the solution to the housing needs of other groups will for the most part lie outside New York City.

The most that the city can do for low-income workers as a distinct group is to support federal legislation which would make it easier to achieve home ownership—specifically by reducing or eliminating the down payment requirement. The city can, and should, however, do much more for the commuting group. It should see that the investments in commuter transportation facilities, which serve as an alternative to housing within the city, are undertaken by the appropriate regional agencies. To be a real alternative, however, these commuter transportation facilities must provide service that is comfortable, quick, and relatively inexpensive. On all three grounds, most of the existing facilities are inadequate. (They provide even less satisfactory service for reverse traffic during rush hours, thus hampering the efforts of the unskilled and semiskilled members of the work force to find employment outside New York City.)

Immediate and effective action to provide better commuter transportation facilities is critical to the future growth of the city and, as must be made clear to surrounding political jurisdictions, to the future growth of the region as a whole. Without better commuter transportation facilities, the city will find it increasingly difficult to attract the caliber of workers essential to the survival and growth of its primary economic activities, and this would be the first step toward the decline of New York City itself. It follows that among the first claims on the city's land resources will be land to provide terminals, if not arteries, for an improved commuter transportation system. The nature of this system will be described below. It is sufficient for now to point out that the city's efforts along these lines will enable it to devote less of its own valuable land resources to residential purposes.

New York may be unable to attract the caliber of labor force required for its primary economic activities not only because of inadequate commuter transportation facilities but also because those who insist on living near their place of employment and can afford to command the necessary space find the city too obnoxious a place in which to live. In this connection, air pollution may represent the greatest threat to New York City—to its growth as an economic entity, as well as to its inhabitants individually—but noise levels and traffic congestion are also tremendous problems. In fact, the whole quality of urban life, and the quality of urban life in New York City especially, must be given continuing close attention.

By taking into account the availability of programs to provide housing for low-income groups in the surrounding suburbs, the adequacy of the commuter transportation network, and the inherent attractiveness of living in New York itself, it should be possible to determine the overall balance of housing required within the five boroughs to assure an adequate work force for the primary economic activities which give New York its comparative advantage over other urban centers. If this amount of housing would not be called forth under the land allocation principle suggested above—even after a maximum investment in commuter transportation facilities—that principle needs to be modified.

A third qualification, a more technical one, involves the specific basis upon which the r.v.a. is to be calculated. The consideration here is not the square footage of space in the building presently occupying a particular parcel of land, but the square footage of space in the building which could be erected on that parcel of land if it were being most effectively utilized. In some parts of the city, the land is occupied by buildings considerably below the height economically feasible if the land were being used for some other purpose. Many of the loft buildings on the streets branching out from Broadway between Canal and 14th Streets fall into this category. In view of the better alternative uses to which these parcels of land could be put, they represent an economically wasteful under-utilization of New York's valuable land resources. To avoid perpetuating this misallocation of municipal assets, it is necessary to compute the r.v.a. on the basis of the square footage of space available if the best use of that land were to be made. While this may be difficult to determine in some cases, a rough estimate of the maximum number of stories should in most instances be possible.

It should be emphasized that the general principle suggested for allocating New York's scarce and valuable space, together with the several qualifications noted, is not a rule to be enacted into law but a working guideline for city agencies, including the New York City Planning Commission. If imaginatively and intelligently applied, it would redound to the benefit of the city not only in the narrow sense of its being an economic enterprise dependent on tax revenues but also in the larger sense of its being the political mechanism by which citizens seek to improve their lives.

While the model of New York City's government as an economic enterprise dependent on tax revenues ignores many of the most important facets of municipal life, it does reflect one essential truth: the level of services which the city is able to provide is limited by the amount of tax-derived income it can command. At the same time, the amount of taxes which the city is able to collect depends on the level of per capita income generated—or what has herein been defined as regional value added per worker. Of the various taxes levied by the city, those whose yields are most directly related to r.v.a. are the several income taxes, including the personal income, the business income, and the public utilities and commercial rent taxes. Together, these taxes account for approximately one-sixth of all revenue collected by the city from local sources (that is, excluding federal and state reimbursements). The yield from the city real estate tax, which accounts for slightly more than half of all revenue collected from local sources, is less directly related to r.v.a. but nevertheless reflects it. The higher the r.v.a., the higher the rentals are likely to be and the higher the assessed value for any particular parcel of land. The yields from the two indirect taxes which the city levies, those on sales and on cigarettes, are also somewhat dependent on r.v.a. If the activities on any parcel of land generate a higher than average r.v.a., they are likely to give rise to higher incomes; and as those connected with the activity have higher incomes, they are likely to spend more money on those items for which sales taxes are collected. These indirect taxes account for slightly more than one-eighth of the revenue obtained from local sources.

Thus, even with its present tax structure, the City of New York will be able to increase its amount of municipal revenue by increasing the r.v.a. While the precise functional relationship between these two variables must still be determined empirically, it should be evident that a strong relationship does exist. As a secondary consideration, it should be noted that a higher r.v.a. will increase the amount of state taxes collected, thereby making more funds available to local communities through various reimbursement programs. At present, state funds finance somewhat less than one-fourth of New York's total operating budget.

Increasing the r.v.a. by the above-suggested land allocation principle will not only serve to increase the city's tax revenues but will also help to alleviate the demands being made on the city for various services. For that principle, if it were followed, would force low-paying industries out of Manhattan, perhaps out of the city entirely. It should be kept in mind that these industries are precisely those which shift part of the burden of maintaining their work force on to the city itself, thereby acting as a drain on municipal revenue.

For many reasons, all deriving from limited space, it is difficult for the individual living in New York City—and in Manhattan, especially—to provide for himself and his family those amenities which have come to be considered an absolute minimum by most Americans. Even the necessities—food, clothing, housing and medical care—can be obtained only at a higher price than in most other communities. The fact that it is more expensive to live in New York City, a fact based on economic realities, suggests that wages and other forms of income for its inhabitants have to be higher. Yet paradoxically wages in many industries, including much of the city's manufacturing sector, are among the lowest in the nation. (There is, of course, the further irony of some persons urging that more low-paying industries be attracted to New York City.) The paradox is understandable only when it is realized that the city government must make up for this deficiency in personal income in various ways.

Since many individuals do not earn enough to pay for their own medical care, the city operates the largest municipal hospital system in the country to provide free or inexpensive health services. Since many of these same persons do not earn enough to afford housing on the open market, the city has set up a separate agency to provide apartments at greatly reduced rents. And since some heads of households do not even earn enough to feed and clothe their families at a subsistence level, the city must dip into its welfare funds to supplement their wages. Certainly these various forms of assistance are humanely motivated and should be continued; indeed they partially serve larger municipal and social objectives. But their cost to the city would be less if these workers could earn higher wages and thus afford to purchase their own necessities. Under the present circumstances, these various forms of assistance are, in part, a subsidy to those industries which pay low wages.

Most of the burden of low wages is borne, however, not

by the city itself, but by the workers. This burden consists of their greatly curtailed material pleasures—the substandard housing, the inadequate diets, the lack of suitable changes of clothing, the inability to get away from the city periodically, the paucity of entertainment, etc. Most of those who receive low wages bear this burden stoically. But some do not. Whether they rebel inwardly by succumbing to various forms of mental illness or whether they rebel outwardly by engaging in various forms of antisocial behavior, the cost of municipal services is increased. This, too, is a form of subsidy to the industries which pay the low wages. While subsidies such as these may well be called for, they should at least be recognized for what they are and weighed against the alternative uses to which the same funds could be put.

If it is in the interest of New York City's government as a business enterprise to have the low-paying industries which occupy the city's scarce and valuable space replaced by activities generating a higher r.v.a., it is even more in the interest of the city as the center of a growing economy. The activities which generate a higher r.v.a. are likely to be those which look not backward to the age of handicraft industry but forward to the age of advanced technological processes. They are, therefore, the activities most likely to serve as the handmaidens of further economic growth. To give an illustration: if a plastics manufacturing firm in Chelsea were replaced by a company turning out software for the electronic data processing industry, the r.v.a. would be increased and the metropolitan region would become more attractive to those economic activities which rely heavily on the new computer technology. Similarly, if the meat-packing establishments in West Harlem were to be replaced by an industrial research complex drawing on the resources and personnel of Columbia University, entirely new industries might eventually be created, further diversifying the already highly diversified economy of the metropolitan region.

While it may be in the interest of the city as a whole to have low-paying industries make room for those which generate a higher r.v.a., it must be recognized that such a move does not necessarily benefit those presently employed by the low-paying industries. Some people will benefit. A certain percentage will undoubtedly be able to find jobs requiring the same skill level in the new activities—and because of the higher r.v.a. they should be better paid, more regularly employed, and perhaps even have a greater chance of moving up the job ladder. Moreover, if the city and other levels of government properly fulfill their training responsibilities, an additional number—or their children—will qualify for the jobs of higher skill level generated by the new activities. But this may still leave many of those formerly employed in the low-wage industries without jobs.

It has already been argued that the low-income groups, those who comprise the bulk of the employment in the low-paying industries, could be better housed if they were to live in suburban communities and commute from there to their jobs in New York City—provided, of course, that the present pattern of residential discrimination could be broken down. It will now be argued that the suburbs, or at least the outer fringes of New York, offer the low-skilled and thus the low-income groups the best hope of meaningful employment, that is, employment which is steady, well paid, and opens up the prospect of advancement. For one thing, such manufacturing activity as is likely to continue to exist in the New York region will be found either in the outlying areas of the city or just beyond, in the suburbs. This is particularly true of the types of manufacturing which offer the most desirable employment opportunities.

Second, the service and retail activities which are dependent on residential demand are likely to continue to be most heavily concentrated in the suburbs, where so many middle- and upper-income families live. These service and retail activities will open up job opportunities, not only for domestic servants but for auto mechanics, municipal employees, and the like. To the extent that there is an unmet demand for the labor of unskilled and semiskilled workers in the metropolitan region, it is most likely to be found in the suburbs.

The obstacles which prevent the exploitation of this source of employment are twofold: an inadequate commuter transportation system and a faulty mechanism for providing job information. (To the extent that low-income groups succeed in establishing residence in the suburbs, these obstacles will be proportionately reduced.) The importance of better commuter transportation has already been discussed. Suffice it to add that, in the past, the major concern of New York City has been that the transportation system enable workers to get to their jobs in the central business district. While this still is essential, it is also important that the system be overhauled so that workers can get to jobs at the fringe of and just outside the city. Up to now, the majority of those forming the reverse commuting group have been individuals able to afford private automobile transportation. If they are to be joined by members of the low-income population, a complementary system of public transportation, perhaps initially subsidized, is mandatory.

So far this chapter has addressed itself to the questions of what the city should do and why. Now it is time to take up the question of how.

The importance of a regional outlook in planning has already been stressed. The necessary mechanisms for achieving this perspective are of two types. The first would be an economic development council on which business and civic leaders from the entire metropolitan region would be asked to serve. On the one hand, this would enable business and civic leaders to become familiar with the factors retarding the economic development of the region. On the other hand, it would go far to assure their support for whatever programs or remedies were devised to overcome the region's problems.

The second mechanism, a regional body bringing together all those involved in planning throughout the region, would be a technical counterpart of the first. At present there are numerous groups, as diverse as the New York City Planning Commission, the Port of New York Authority, the First National City Bank, the New York Central Railroad, and the Northern Valley Regional Planning Committee in New Jersey, all independently trying to plan for the future. What is needed is some mechanism for coordinating, but not controlling, their disparate efforts. In addition to providing a point of contact for these various local planning groups, a regional planning coordinating council would serve as an advisory body to the regional economic development council, with responsibility to point out the problems confronting the region and to explore the practicability of the solutions suggested.

The role of New York City officials should be to provide the impetus for the creation of both types of councils. It will be noted that the proposed mechanisms for cooperation are at the nongovernmental level, and this should allay some of the political opposition to regional efforts of this type. If the two councils fulfill their function effectively, more formal governmental cooperation may not be necessary.

Among the first problems which an economic development council should take up is that of better integrating the commuter transportation within the region. (Seeing that the necessary investments are made in long-distance transportation facilities—specifically, in containerized vessel berths and a fourth jet airport—should also be among the council's first tasks.) A solution to the commuter transportation problem could proceed along the following lines:

a. The purchase by a transportation authority of the rights-of-way of all railroads serving the area.

b. The delegation of power to the authority to establish rates and schedules for all passenger movements; and provision to the authority of financial flexibility and subsidies to assure that it can maintain an adequate level of service.

While some progress along these lines has already been made by the states of New York and New Jersey individually, this represents only the beginning of what must be done to create a rational, integrated commuter transportation system. Once the regional economic development council and the subsidiary planning coordinating body have been created, city officials should insist that the commutation problems be given first priority for consideration.

Within the city itself, the most pressing need is to establish the principle of land allocation discussed above as municipal policy. It should be reflected in both the zoning decisions of the City Planning Commission and in the local taxes which the mayor asks the City Council to approve.

Afterword: A Manpower Strategy

THIS Afterword will pull together the principal findings that can be extracted from the foregoing chapters to help fashion a manpower strategy for the metropolis. Since the analysis covered a wide terrain, since the chapters pursued different approaches, and since they did not always lead to similar conclusions, it might be well to make explicit here the areas of consensus about the forces that are shaping the metropolitan economy, the policies and programs that offer the greatest prospect of maintaining that the city's vitality, and the organizational structures and relationships that must be strengthened or established to assure that a policy for growth can be effectively implemented.

Understanding the City's Manpower Problems

The quarter of a century since World War II has unleashed many new forces and has reinforced earlier trends that have altered the structure and functioning of the nation's major metropolises. From the present analysis, which has been focused on the manpower dimensions of this revolution, the important findings are:

1. A continuing and rapid erosion of the comparative advantages of many of the nation's largest cities and simul-

taneous accelerated growth of smaller cities. Since a slower rate of growth, stability, or decline of the economy makes adjustments between the labor force and the job market more difficult, the mismatching of men and jobs has been accentuated in the slower-growing major metropolises.

2. The flight to the outlying regions of white middle-class families from all metropolitan areas together with the relocation of many enterprises, from manufacturing to retailing, has further contributed to this mismatching. As many of the established urban groups became suburbanites, migrants from the South and from Puerto Rico moved into the central cities in search of jobs and a new life. Since municipal authorities were unable or unwilling to enforce the building codes, the numbers who squeezed into the vacated space exceeded the numbers who had left, with the result that buildings and neighborhoods deteriorated. This in turn exerted pressure on the remaining white families to follow the move to the suburbs. In this major reshuffling of populations, the major cities of the North and West were filled with in-migrants who were poorly prepared for the complexities of urban life. One consequence was the substantial increase in welfare and related costs that had to be met by municipal government; because of the consequent high taxes, the city became a less-attractive place for many business enterprises.

3. This was not, of course, the first time in the development of the United States that cities received large numbers of immigrants and in-migrants who were handicapped in adjusting to urban life and work. But there were some important differences between the recent and the older streams. A high proportion of the recent newcomers are Negroes who were subjected to much more severe discrim-

ination in jobs, housing, and all other aspects of living than were the immigrants of an earlier day. Moreover, the city, which until World War I had had a great many jobs for unskilled workers, now was hospitable primarily only to professional, technical, and other types of white-collar workers. The outmigration of many enterprises in manufacturing and trade had reduced the number of blue-collar jobs in the central city. Hence it became much more difficult in recent years to match the new in-migrants with the available jobs.

4. The experience of Western Europe since the end of World War II teaches that among the principal reasons that New York and other American cities have had such difficulties in absorbing the new in-migrants into profitable employment has been the generally slack level of demand for labor during most of the last quarter of a century. Except during the early 1940s, and again at the height of the Korean War, the level of unemployment and underemployment has been markedly higher in the United States than in Western Europe. Those who have the least to offer employers are those most likely to be in the peripheral labor force—minority groups, women, and old persons.

5. Much effort and money has been directed during the past years to programs aimed at removing or alleviating the handicaps of the poorly endowed and poorly trained in the hope and expectation of improving their prospects for employment. But as several of the contributors to this book have stressed, there are narrow limits within which such a policy can operate. If the total demand for labor remains slack, improving the qualifications of one part of the supply will simply result in their advancing in the queue. Another group will become the last hired, first fired. Moreover, since there are limited prospects for advancement for many who

are regularly employed, it is difficult for the less qualified to get and hold a job, particularly a good job.

6. The shift from manufacturing to service jobs in metropolitan employment has resulted in the availability of a large number of low-paying, dead-end, and intermittent work opportunities for the poorly educated and trained. One of the challenges facing the metropolis is to improve its overall job structure so that only a small minority must hold these jobs. Since many young Negroes who enter the labor market have little opportunity to get a job other than one which pays little, has little status, and offers few if any prospects for advancement, this unquestionably adds to the alienation of these young people and to their frustration and hostility.

7. The difficulties of absorbing poorly educated and poorly trained young people and adults into the urban economy have been accentuated, as we have seen, by the flight of many enterprises to outlying areas in search of more suitable land, lower taxes, and better access to transportation networks. The impact of various technological developments—particularly those associated with the automobile and the truck—has been to speed decentralization. One of the most important suggestions advanced in the preceding analysis was the possibility of a new turn in technology which may lead to a reversal of this trend when important advantages may once again accrue to those who decide to locate, remain, or expand their operations within the city proper. Although the balance between the powerful forces which still pull enterprises to the periphery and the new forces which may start to pull them to the center is hard to determine, the fact that technology may contribute anew to

centralization is an important finding for those who must plan for tomorrow.

8. Since the core city is ineluctably linked to the suburbs and since the economic well-being of one is closely linked to the prosperity of the other, it is essential that transportation networks be improved so that the present difficulties in bringing people and jobs together are reduced. In this connection attention must be directed to reverse transportation movements, that is, to enabling ghetto populations to travel to the suburbs easily and cheaply so that they will have greater access to the blue-collar and service jobs that are available there. The rate of expansion on the peripheries of cities will be slowed unless the available labor force within the city can be tapped.

9. Most of the findings recapitulated here have dealt with the problems connected with successfully absorbing the poorly educated in an increasingly sophisticated urban economy in which many of the fastest growing areas require primarily only professional, technical, and other types of white-collar workers. The vitality of cities depends in considerable measure on solving the problems of the hard-to-employ and in assuring that new and expanding enterprises have ready access to large numbers of trained persons to fill the ever larger proportion of managerial and technical positions. Since this supply is crucial for the continued growth and prosperity of the urban economy, the size and strength of the educational and training facilities within the metropolitan area are of paramount significance. The city, which has many junior colleges, colleges, technical institutes, universities, and other facilities to produce a large number of educated and trained personnel in a wide range

of fields will have a distinct advantage over other cities which have fewer educational facilities.

The contribution of higher education to the urban economy must be assessed not only from the viewpoint of the number of regularly enrolled students pursuing an undergraduate or graduate degree but also in terms of its contribution to the large numbers in the community who must pursue their studies on a part-time basis because they must work, keep house, or fulfill some other commitment.

10. People work in the city, others live in it, some come for recreational purposes, others to study, some to seek medical treatment. Whether those who come to the city stay for a short time or remain permanently; whether they opt to work there and whether they also make their homes there depends in considerable measure on the quality of the urban environment relative to the realistic alternatives. We know that a great many families have decided that they will not live in the city even if they work there. We know further that while many are attracted to the city, others are repelled by the dirt, the noise, the congestion, and the lack of personal safety. The metropolis cannot offer all the advantages of cosmopolitan living and at the same time provide the amenities that attach to small-town life. Some of the consequences of density—the essence of metropolitanism—are inevitable. But it does not follow that the urban environment need deteriorate to a point where people are frightened to walk the streets, where the public schools are shunned by parents with college-bound children, or where transportation is an ordeal.

There is no point in trying to solve a large number of specific manpower problems, ranging from jobs for the hard-to-employ to an adequate flow of talent and competence, and including additional challenges such as the effective use of educated women, the reduction of peripherality in employment, and the provision of meaningful career opportunities to young workers, or to concentrate on answers to these admittedly high priority problems, if we continue to neglect the overriding issue of how the city can maintain its attractiveness to the many groups of able and energetic people who are the keystone to its vitality and prosperity. The fact that a high proportion of these people are unwilling to live in the city is warning that, if the urban environment continues to deteriorate, they may refuse to work there. This threat must be recognized, met, and turned back. A successful manpower strategy for the metropolis must be tested by using the simple criterion that able people can see their future as urbanites. Every program and policy must be weighed on this scale.

Policies and Programs

Each of the foregoing chapters concludes with a list of recommendations for action which the city should undertake to assure that its economy remains vibrant and that its people have good jobs and incomes. In this summary, we will present the most important of these suggestions for public and private action at the metropolitan level.

First, we will note briefly the range of actions that falls within the domain of the federal government. While we must not overlook the scope for constructive action that lies within the competence of a local population, we must not assume that major cities can, on their own, solve their economic and manpower problems. They cannot.

The authors of the several chapters repeatedly directed

attention to the critical role that a sustained high demand for labor plays in contributing to the more effective utilization of manpower resources. If the labor market is slack, as it has been throughout so many of the postwar years, it is inevitable that considerable numbers of persons within the labor force and on the periphery, such as young people, married women, and older persons, will be unemployed, underemployed, or will not even look for a job although they want and need one.

It is generally agreed in this post-Keynesian world that the maintenance of a generally high level of unemployment is the clear responsibility of the federal government. It is less clear, however, whether the federal government can reduce the unemployment rates, as currently calculated, below the 4 percent level through reliance on general fiscal and monetary policy without generating serious inflationary pressures. If the country can presently provide more jobs only at the cost of rising prices, the federal government must explore alternatives that may accomplish the first without the second. Congress is slowly edging up to serious consideration of a major job creation program to help absorb many of the unemployed or underemployed, particularly in ghetto areas. Although the Clark-Prouty Bill was not passed in the Senate in the fall of 1967, the margin of defeat was small. In the months and years ahead, it should become increasingly clear to the federal lawmakers that they must confront, albeit belatedly, the challenge of fulfilling the implicit commitment of the Employment Act of 1946 to provide opportunities for employment for all who are able and willing to work.

Since 1962 the federal government, particularly through the Manpower Development and Training Act and the programs of the Office of Economic Opportunity, has made sizable sums available to improve the capabilities of the hard-to-employ in the hope and expectation that through literacy and skill-training their employability would be enhanced. Many who were trained obtained jobs for which they otherwise would not have qualified. But a training approach can be successful only if the number of potential jobs equals the number of potential job seekers, and only if training opportunities are available for all who want and need them.

We have noted that there has been a shortfall of jobs in the economy. Now we must add that there has been a substantial shortfall of good training slots. A rough calculation of the gap between the need for and availability of training opportunities in New York City in 1966 indicates a ratio of 6 to 1. Moreover, the administrative relations among the federal government, the state, and the localities have been so cumbersome that the potential effectiveness of the federal dollars has been greatly reduced. If training can contribute significantly to raising the level of manpower utilization in the nation's major cities—and it unquestionably can—better policy, more funds, and greater involvement of community leadership is required.

An unique dimension of the large concentrations of hard-to-employ in the ghetto areas of the cities of the North and West is that so many Negroes and Puerto Ricans are among the in-migrants who have relocated from farms, towns, and small cities. The failure of the federal government to mount significant programs to help prepare these migrants prior to or after their relocation has meant that their difficulties in sinking roots in their new metropolitan environment have been unmitigated and in turn their new neighbors have found it difficult to adjust to them. The large-scale movement of people across state lines calls for federal assistance even if state and local governments must also be involved in the process.

The federal government has long been involved in highways and housing and recently in interurban transportation. But the record suggests that the federal government is only belatedly becoming aware of the importance of using its great powers to encourage planning for the entire metropolitan area in such fashion that the needs and interests of minority groups are not disregarded or sacrificed for the benefit of other stronger members of the community. To rebuild the central city at the expense of uprooting the poor, to use federal funds so that discrimination in housing in the suburbs is reinforced, to build highways that destroy the enterprises which provide jobs for the unskilled and semi-skilled, these elements of federal policy in the past have made the minority poor pay for whatever urban progress we have seen. Recently, the terms of federal grants for metropolitan planning and action have included criteria which show more sensitivity for the economic and social needs of low-income and minority groups. But the scale of federal funds remains much too small. The urban environment continues to deteriorate at a rate faster than remedial action is instituted.

Recently, the federal government has begun to take an active interest in mass interurban transportation, which is at the heart of metropolitan planning. Congress has made some small appropriations. But here too we are still losing ground.

While much more federal assistance will have to be forthcoming on both the housing and transportation fronts, the states and localities can do, and are doing, a great deal to help themselves. This, is also true about other aspects of the urban environment such as air and water pollution. Federal involvement in these areas must grow, but the other units of government also have an important role to play.

We have seen that the cities of tomorrow require a much larger federal involvement to create and maintain a viable, physical, social, and economic environment. The following paragraphs will set forth the lines of action that can and must be taken by local leadership, both public and private, if the large metropolis is to remain a viable community. Again within the context of this analysis, emphasis will be on how the city's manpower resources can be more effectively trained and more productively employed.

1. Only 60 percent of the age-relevant population in New York City graduate from high school. When we add to the 40 percent who drop out the considerable group who have learned little although they have acquired a high-school diploma, it is clear that the city's schools are not adequately preparing young people for the world of work. This is not to say that there is no future for the high-school dropout, but that such high drop-out rates are prima facie cause for concern in an overwhelmingly service economy in which communication and quantitative skills loom increasingly important. High on the city's agenda is to make the necessary changes in the shortest possible time to enable the education system to do its job. New York's economy and society will deteriorate a generation hence if the schools continue to pour into the labor market so many young people who are unprepared to find meaningful jobs that will enable them to advance and achieve security.

2. While concern with those still in the school system is

important, the large numbers of younger people who have passed through it and are now struggling to make a place for themselves in the economy and society must not be disregarded. There are a great many, with varying degrees of educational achievement, who, as they mature, realize that they have need for more education and training. While New York has a tremendous array of public and private educational and training facilities, there are still unmet needs for free and low-cost adult educational and training opportunities for the high-school and college drop-out. A major challenge to community leadership is to identify these deficiencies and to act to remedy them forthwith.

3. The fact that so many youths have left high school without acquiring a diploma and the certainty that this pattern will continue for many years to come, although we hope that the proportion will decline, makes it essential that municipal government restudy its hiring requirements to determine the relevance of its standards and to lower them when indicated. Once its own house is in order in this regard, it should encourage private and nonprofit employers to do likewise. The maintenance of artificially high standards has been demonstrated to be a serious cost not only to the potential worker but also to the employer.

4. Since the dynamic sectors of the city have an unmet need for people with high orders of ability and competence, the large pool of educated women represents an important potential asset. However, to tap it effectively will require adjustments along a great many fronts: in colleges and universities to facilitate the entry and reentry of women into degree and nondegree programs; in the provision, under public, nonprofit, and private auspices, of competent guidance and placement services; by employers in scheduling; in

the expansion of child-care facilities; and in opening company training and promotion opportunities to able women.

5. Over 70 percent of all jobs in New York City are in the service sector of the economy. Many of these jobs pay poorly and worse; they are not part of a job hierarchy; a man entering at the bottom can look forward only to the same low-level job or leaving. Effective manpower utilization requires that men be afforded an opportunity to learn while they work and an opportunity to be promoted as they acquire competence. Hence it is incumbent upon all employers, private, nonprofit, and governmental, to restudy their job ladders and to provide for orderly progression. In this connection, unions can and should advise employers of the desires and needs of workers for in-service and extramural training opportunities.

6. Almost 6 percent of all jobs in New York are in the health services industry, and it is likely that this proportion will grow under the forced draft of Medicare and Medicaid as well as the willingness of the consumer to spend more of his income on health care. The health field has provided employment opportunities for the poorly educated and trained as well as for those in the top professional ranks. Despite the rapid growth of employment in the health field, many manpower shortages exist and more are anticipated. The ability of New York to maintain its leadership position in this industry will depend in part on its willingness and determination to improve its training and utilization practices. The high density of medical installations within the city provides an excellent opportunity for rationalizing and improving the training that is now carried on largely under the auspices of individual hospitals. The City University and the community colleges have begun to move into the field,

but much more can be done to bring all of the involved educational institutions into a more integrated plan, to determine by agreement the fields of specialization for the several colleges and universities, and to improve the relations between them and the service institutions which must continue to provide opportunities for clinical and laboratory experience. Employment can be increased through cooperation among the Hospital Association, the several trade unions, and the professional associations. Here is a splintered market that can be greatly strengthened through cooperative arrangements which will redound to the advantage of the workers, the employers, and the public. Part of any effort at rationalization should be a hard look at present standards for certification and, equally important, a determination of how ways can be made to enable people to advance up the skill hierarchy as they acquire greater competence on the job or through additional education.

7. The cutting edge of modern industry is the research and development laboratory; therefore, the city with ready access to large numbers of educated and trained persons has an advantage. The large higher educational structure of New York City and environs together with its significant number of nonprofit foundations and research laboratories is a major asset. The many corporate headquarters and industrial laboratories in the area is another source of strength. Yet the full exploitation of these assets requires more planning and coordination than has as yet been accomplished, when all the initiative has been left to the individual enterprise to tap into the rich human resources pool. There is no agency, governmental or other, that is concerned with a closer correlation between the emergent needs of enterprise, and the best ways of meeting them from

among the strong scientific and research resources of New York. For instance, no one agency is concerned with the attraction to the city of more federal research and development grants, or with determining the steps that must be taken by the community in anticipation of expanding one or another of its research functions. There is no leadership clearly responsible for assuring that the research potential of the city is effectively husbanded and utilized.

While there are councils and committees that provide for some interchange between the public and private institutions of higher learning, both within the city proper and in the metropolitan area, a strong planning and research effort aimed at correlating the growth and specialization of the two types of institutions cannot be mounted at present because of inadequate structure and staffing.

8. Two major factors have contributed to weakening the city's ability to provide jobs for all its people, particularly those with little education or skill. One is the absence of effective transportation links between where the poor reside and the jobs which they could fill. More attention must be directed by municipal authorities to improving transportation from the core city to the periphery so that the ghetto populations have greater opportunity to find work. This involves both reliable transportation and cost. If a man must spend inordinate amounts of time getting to and from a job, or if he must allocate to traveling a disproportionate amount of his earnings, he will not even begin to search for employment far from his home.

To improve the linkages between minority groups in the inner city and jobs on the periphery, responsible government agencies must be informed about where employment is expanding, where employers are most pressed for additional workers, and how the available transportation network might be supplemented (usually by an additional bus line) in order to bring potential employees to the jobs. Equally important is the establishment of a reasonable fare, which might require a partial subsidy. In instances of acute labor shortages, it might be possible for the city to interest a group of employers to contribute to the subsidy. Without special and continuing efforts on the part of the municipal officials to move into the breach, the non-fit between stranded workers and available jobs is likely to persist.

Municipal officialdom must also develop sophistication in the assembling, zoning, and leasing or selling of land within its borders. No resource is more scarce within a city; no resource requires more careful handling to make its maximum contribution to the continued vitality of the urban economy. A dynamic city needs a balanced population for the expansion of high wage-employment and for the growth of strategically important social overhead structures—from universities to hospitals. To achieve this end, the proper planning and control of its land is the most critical challenge facing the municipal authorities. As with every facet of planning, the responsible officials can make major contributions by innovations. Planning for better land use would involve the collection of discrete parcels into larger units for special purposes; the exploitation of air rights; fill-ins along the water front; and above all the stimulation of public-private cooperation for large-scale, industrial, residential, and service developments. Neither government nor private enterprise alone is likely to be able to raise the sums required to transform deteriorated areas into vital neighborhoods, but together they can do a great deal.

9. The pull of the city is strong because it offers an excit-

ing life. The density of population has facilitated the specialization of functions that has underpinned economic growth and development, and it has also provided the base for a wide range of activities that depend on the proximity of large numbers who share goals and objectives. But density brings costs as well as gains, and lately the costs have risen to a point where many who want to work and live in large cities have had second thoughts. Among the worst drawbacks have been dirty air, dirty streets, slow traffic, crimes of violence, group antagonisms, poor public services, and other dangers, difficulties, and annoyances which have convinced increasing numbers of Americans that the city is a bad environment for children and a questionable environment for themselves.

To say that more policemen should patrol the streets is easy. But how can this be done without increasing taxes? And if taxes go up, will it not encourage the exodus of various enterprises, with the result that the tax base will shrink and compound the difficulties of raising revenue for essential services? To take another example: if the proportion of children from racial and ethnic minorities increases to where the public school is predominantly nonwhite, the removal of the remaining white children is likely to be accelerated. If that occurs, white middle-class families with children will not want to remain in a city where their own children will constitute a minority.

There is no single group which alone can reverse these trends. The protection of sound neighborhoods and the rehabilitation of deteriorated neighborhoods requires the cooperation of all who live and work in the city. Employers, trade unions, churches, large voluntary organizations—all who have a stake in the viability and vitality of the city—

must be able and willing to participate in the fashioning of policies and programs that can contribute to the well-being of the metropolis.

Implicit in such cooperation is the willingness of all key groups to work toward the speedy dissolution of the rigid demarcations that still prevail in all American cities between the Negro minority and the white majority. No city can look forward to the future with equanimity if present patterns of segregation and discrimination are maintained. They represent a cancer that can undermine even the strongest city. The strength of a metropolis is grounded on the free and willing cooperation of all who live therein. If a significant minority is denied the opportunity to participate fully in the life of the city, it will sooner or later undermine the health of the entire metropolis. Those who are concerned about the city of tomorrow must make possible the participation of the excluded minority today.

These considerations do not relate only to the city proper. The city can no longer be left to struggle alone with the multiple problems of the minority poor while the white middle- and upper-income classes retreat to the suburbs after work, to live unconcerned and undisturbed by the unsolved problems of the metropolis. Those who earn their livelihood in the city must help in the solution of these problems, else their own livelihood is in jeopardy. The artificial separation of city and suburb must be broken down. The man who works in the city during the day and sleeps in suburbia is a citizen of the metropolitan area.

10. We do not now have the political instrumentalities to reunite city and suburb. Only a beginning has been made through the establishment of regional planning bodies, and interstate compacts involving basic services

such as water, sewage, transportation. We do not even have in the city proper the instrumentalities to assure effective cooperation between the private, nonprofit, and governmental sectors. This is an essential first step, since all of the strengths of the metropolis must be harnessed if its survival and prosperity are to be assured. We need new and effective mechanisms to relate the central city to its satellite communities, so that the actions of one can be assessed in terms of the consequences on the other.

New and improved relations must be established between the city and the metropolitan region and state government. Similarly, many problems can be resolved only as adjoining states develop new and effective ways of jointly assessing and solving problems that confront their separate areas.

Recently the federal government has begun to develop new mechanisms for assisting the metropolises where so many of the nation's acute problems are centered. The metropolises certainly need the assistance of the federal government, but many problems remain to be resolved, particularly how the new federal-municipal relations can be articulated within the traditional system.

Manpower strategy for the metropolis can be successful only if two developments take place. First, every city must develop a research potential so that it can assess emerging economic trends and weigh the policy alternatives among which it must choose. Second, a successful manpower strategy requires the establishment and elaboration of more effective mechanisms for policy assessment and determination at every level—city, metropolitan area, state, region, nation, and, equally important, effective coordination among these several instrumentalities.

We can no longer take for granted the economic well-being of metropolitan America. Since three-quarters of the total population will soon live within these metropolitan areas, the future of the country depends on our ability to meet and solve the key problems confronting the cities. Research and organization are essential ingredients of a successful strategy.

A successful strategy for the metropolis requires that all who live therein play a part in fashioning it, and that all who will be affected by it have an opportunity to profit from it. The strength of a metropolis is that the whole can utilize the contribution of each member and that each member in turn can draw strength from the whole.

Bibliography

THE larger investigations that underlie each of the chapters are noted below. Unless otherwise indicated, all books are or will be published by the Columbia University Press.

1. *Patterns of Employment Expansion in the American Economy.* Thomas M. Stanback and Richard V. Knight. 1969.
2. *Electronic Data Processing in New York City: Lessons for Metropolitan Economics.* Boris Yavitz and Thomas M. Stanback. 1967.
3. *Manpower and the Growth of Producer Services.* Harry I. Greenfield. 1966.
4. *Allied Health Manpower.* Harry I. Greenfield with Carol A. Brown. 1968.
5. *Educational Requirements for Employment.* Ivar E. Berg with Sherry Gorelick. New York, Center for Urban Education, 1968.
6. *Process of Work Attachment.* Marcia K. Freedman. 1968.
7. *The Peripheral Worker.* Dean Morse. 1968.
8. *The Hard-to-Employ: European Experience.* Beatrice G. Reubens. 1968.
9. *Life Styles of Educated Women.* Eli Ginzberg and Associates. 1966.
10. *Career Changes in the Middle Years.* Dale L. Hiestand. 1969.
11. *State Development Efforts to Expand Employment.* Alfred S. Eichner. 1969.

Index